THE
NEW
ENTREPRENEURS

THE
NEW
ENTREPRENEURS

BUILDING A GREEN
ECONOMY FOR THE FUTURE

ANDREW
HEINTZMAN

ANANSI

This edition published in 2010 by
House of Anansi Press Inc.
110 Spadina Avenue, Suite 801
Toronto, ON, M5V 2K4
Tel. 416-363-4343
Fax 416-363-1017
www.anansi.ca

Distributed in Canada by
HarperCollins Canada Ltd.
1995 Markham Road
Scarborough, ON, M1B 5M8
Toll free tel. 1-800-387-0117

Distributed in the United States by
Publishers Group West
1700 Fourth Street
Berkeley, CA 94710
Toll free tel. 1-800-788-3123

House of Anansi Press is committed to protecting our natural environment. As part of our efforts, this book is printed on paper that contains 100% post-consumer recycled fibres, is acid-free, and is processed chlorine-free.

14 13 12 11 10   1 2 3 4 5

Library and Archives Canada Cataloguing in Publication

Heintzman, Andrew, 1967–
The new entrepreneurs / Andrew Heintzman.

Includes index.

ISBN 978-0-88784-227-6

1. Green technology — Economic aspects — Canada. 2. Technological innovations — Environmental aspects — Canada. 3. Clean energy industries — Canada. 4. Entrepreneurship — Canada. 5. New business enterprises — Canada. I. Title.

HD62.5.H45 2010   338.9'270971   C2009-906503-7

Library of Congress Control Number: 2010923894

Jacket design: Bill Douglas
Text design and typesetting: Sari Naworynski

Canada Council   Conseil des Arts   ONTARIO ARTS COUNCIL
for the Arts   du Canada   CONSEIL DES ARTS DE L'ONTARIO

We acknowledge for their financial support of our publishing program the Canada Council for the Arts, the Ontario Arts Council, and the Government of Canada through the Canada Book Fund.

Printed and bound in Canada

For Roz, Theodore, and Molly

CONTENTS

And the story is told
Of human veins and pulses,
Of eternal pathways of fire,
Of dreams that survive the night,
Of doors held ajar in storms.
    F. J. Pratt, "Newfoundland"

If you look at the science about what is happening on
earth and aren't pessimistic, you don't understand the
data. But if you meet the people who are working to
restore this earth and the lives of the poor, and you
aren't optimistic, you haven't got a pulse.
    Paul Hawken, Commencement Address
    to the University of Portland, Class of 2009

PREFACE

FIFTEEN YEARS AGO I READ a book that set me on a new path.

I was at my parents' farm, and my brother Tom was reading Paul Hawken's *The Ecology of Commerce*, the bestselling book about the environment, business, and economic reform. I was interested in the subject, and on my request Tom read some passages from the book to me. I have to admit it — my first reaction was that Hawken's view of the world sounded unrelentingly gloomy: the ocean was being fished out; we were double-glazing the atmosphere with carbon; species were going extinct at record rates. At first, this gloominess didn't correspond with what I saw around me. It was 1995. The economy was bouncing back from a recession; the technology revolution was well underway, opening up a whole new world of communication; the Iron Curtain had fallen and democracy was on the march; the world was relatively peaceful. In short, things were good. So why was this environmentalist raining on the parade?

Fortunately, this knee-jerk reaction did not prevent me from reading the book, which had a profound effect on me and fundamentally altered my perspective. What the book taught me was that an essential connection between the environment and the economy had been severed to the detriment of both. Hawken had identified a significant problem, perhaps *the* problem of our time: a design flaw in our economic system had allowed capitalism to become wasteful and inevitably unsustainable. And this design flaw was driving us toward a crisis that previously I had not seen clearly, but thereafter I could not ignore. More importantly, Hawken had also described a way to reconcile the interests of environmentalism and economics. And that was through the emergence of a new kind of capitalism.

Reading the book was a revelation. By showing how the environment and the economy can — indeed, must — be reconciled, he revealed how the deepest wound in our modern society could be healed. In this respect, what I realized was that far from being gloomy, Hawken was articulating a powerfully positive message. The book made such an impression on me that I bought twenty extra copies and sent them to important corporate and political leaders. Finance minister Paul Martin received a copy. So did Bill Gates. I kept thinking to myself: if just one of these über powerful people heard the message, we could change the world. Most sent polite form letters in reply, but Martin's office, to his credit, actually called and asked for further reading.

Happily, I came to realize that a groundswell of people were already trying to use capitalism to solve environmental problems. These people were mostly entrepreneurs, developing small businesses that would provide low-impact energy, water purification systems, and models of sustainable agriculture. I became convinced that reconciling the split that Hawken had described lay primarily in the hands of these entrepreneurs.

So I helped to start a company that would invest in these businesses and support these entrepreneurs. At the time it was considered a radical idea. The investment industry was inclined to see these companies as highly marginal. And so it took a number of years to raise the initial capital required for a fund, but eventually my partners and I were able to do so. Over the last eight years I have spent my days seeking out green companies with high-profit potential. We have now invested in ten environmental companies — some of which are described in the pages of this book.

These companies and sectors have since moved out of the margins. Governments, financial institutions, and the public recognize that they are providing solutions to many of the greatest problems we have today. They not only rise to Paul Hawken's challenge — to define a new kind of capitalism that reconciles environmental and economic values — but they are also advancing the inevitable goal of capitalists: to make money doing so.

HUMAN HISTORY IS MARKED by periods of profound and dramatic change, in which the methods of previous generations give way to new strategies. These moments are often the result of technological innovations that open up new possibilities and render older systems obsolete. Sometimes they come as a result of new ways of organizing society: novel political or economic structures, for example. Alternatively, they may be driven by a moral imperative, where new value systems force a change; the end of slavery is an example of how new social values played an important role in the broad evolution of society. When all of these imperatives are aligned — as they are today — then the most dramatic transformations become possible, and perhaps inevitable.

We are now in the midst of a great societal shift, a time of fundamental change driven by the strains of a rapidly growing population consuming an ever greater amount of resources on a finite planet. The ultimate cause and expression of this fissure is how we use our natural resources — the biophysical substrata such as forests, water, air, atmosphere, minerals, fuel, biodiversity, soil — which are essential to our lives and the ultimate source of all our wealth.

Over the last two hundred years a startling age of invention has resulted in the depletion of ancient stores of resources in the geological equivalent of a blink of an eye. New tools have provided humanity with the means to thrive as never before, allowing populations to grow exponentially and thus exacerbating the incredible drawdown of our natural capital. This unparalleled resource binge is the defining characteristic of the last two hundred years of planet Earth. The next two hundred years will be very different, for we will need to adapt in order to avoid breaching the limits of the natural world.

Our capitalist economic system has hastened this moment, placing extraordinary value on generating material goods for consumption far beyond what is required for sustaining our quality of life. And governments have stood passively by, or even facilitated this imbalance, by allowing the consequences and costs of our wastefulness to go unconsidered. So we have lived beyond our means, outside of the constraints of all previous ages. Just as we now see that financial debt can ruin a household or a country, we are beginning to understand that another debt has been inexorably building. The depletion of our natural capital is in effect a debt we have left to future generations, which they will be forced to repay either by replenishing our natural capital or through a diminished standard of living.

But our economic system also carries the seed of reconciliation. Capitalism is a powerful engine of change, capable of facilitating incredible transformations. We need only look back at the past century, for example, to remember how quickly the world changed with the development of the automobile or computers. And we now have the opportunity to use our stunning technological know-how to usher in a new era of innovation, broader than what has come before and more focused on providing true wealth and health to our societies. Capitalism — put to the task of reducing our use of resources and preserving natural capital — has an almost unlimited potential to alter the way we live.

As our environmental challenges mount, there is an urgent need for leadership to show a way for society to move onto a more sustainable path. It has been assumed — wrongly, I think — that that leadership must come from a politician. The idea of a single individual capable of leading society through the wilderness like a modern-day Moses is an attractive notion. But it may not be realistic. Our current political leaders, even great ones, are encumbered by the inevitable failings of the political process. Burdened by the short-term thinking that results from our electoral process and the confrontational nature of the political theatre, they struggle to move society forward in any far-reaching way. We need to look somewhere else for leadership.

In our capitalist society, the primary agent and catalyst for change is the entrepreneur. A hybrid character, the entrepreneur has the innovation of the inventor, the persuasion of a salesman, the leadership of a politician, the practicality of an investor, the vision of an artist, the nerves of a fighter pilot, and the faith of a priest. Through their industry, they alter the material conditions of the society they live in, a society which must now account for its own excesses. They are working already, in great numbers and with remarkable passion, taking extraordinary risks to usher us along a new path. Because they work independently — each focusing on a separate issue — we may overlook their transformative potential. My goal here is to take a step back and show

how these entrepreneurs are working together as a collective on different pieces of a joint endeavour. I believe that when we see things in that way, we will then understand this transformative potential.

For Canada, the preservation of natural capital is of special urgency, because we are blessed with so much of the world's biological and life-supporting potential, and because our economy to a great extent has been built upon the extraction of these valuable resources. But this good fortune also conveys a special responsibility. And despite our self-image, the reality is that we have not been good stewards. So the need to fashion a more sustainable society becomes increasingly urgent in the coming years, in part because of the greater focus and attention placed on global climate change.

For Canada, climate change poses a number of unique challenges. As a northern country, our landscape and geography will be more affected by rising temperatures than most countries. As a decentralized political entity with natural resources spread unevenly across different provinces and territories, the impact of climate change will tear dangerously at our delicate political fabric. And as a country that sees itself as a force for good in the world, the dawning realization that we have landed squarely on the wrong side of the biggest issue of our time will continue to undermine our self-identity, our self-respect, and our stature on the world's stage. But the greatest impact of climate change will be on our economy. Canada is a vast, cold country highly reliant on cheap energy. In order to reduce our greenhouse gas emissions, new constraints in the form of increased costs and reduced consumption will inevitably be imposed on our energy. And these constraints may place new challenges on our economy. But as I will show, these challenges are, in the end, temporary, and adapting to climate change will present more economic benefits than drawbacks.

Our ancestors faced great hazards and challenges in building this country, and took great risks. Through sheer effort they built the institutions that we have inherited: the industries, the political systems, the universities, the cities, and the railways that have come to define the nation. But the foundation on which they built these institutions is no longer viable, and so we must now seek a new economic model in order to move forward.

I will argue that for the nation to succeed, it will require on the one hand building on something old, and on the other creating something very new. In essence, we must rediscover the entrepreneurial spirit that helped establish the great institutions and enterprises of the country, but we need to do so in a way that is antithetical to the one that built this country in the first place. Our ancestors founded a society based on the assumption that the natural resources around them — the fish, forests, minerals, beaver, bison, oil, coal, and rivers — were virtually limitless. Today we must mobilize this same entrepreneurial spirit, but we must do so based on the realization that those natural resources do have limits.

My goal in the first chapter is to show how the assumption of a zero net sum relationship between the environment and the economy is a false choice. Dealing with environmental problems can lead to economic growth. I will argue that environmental stresses cause real economic costs, and factoring in the limits of natural capital into the economy will lead to greater investment in innovation and technology, resulting in increased productivity and economic growth. In the subsequent chapters, I will show how these opportunities are expressing themselves through a variety of sectors, by introducing the reader to the many entrepreneurs who are creating exciting new technologies and companies to build a more sustainable society.

My aim is to show how we have it in our power — both as individuals and as a collective — to succeed in remaking our economy in a world of ecological constraints. And while this project won't come without risks and challenges, no country is more able: blessed with unmatched wealth, education, and resources, Canada is in a position to become a model for sustainable economic prosperity.

Throughout the book I will introduce you to some of the people I have met who are part of a larger movement to build a green economy. I hope their stories will inspire others, and will help to tell the tale of an economy and a society in transition. Some of the businesses will likely achieve commercial success. Some will not succeed, which is an inevitable part of life for many early-stage companies. But whether or not they meet their commercial goals, all of these entrepreneurs and companies are helping to define an important evolution in the Canadian economy. And in that respect they are all part of a bigger picture.

I have the space and time to write only about a small number of these admirable people. There are many others who have not made it into these pages and who are equally notable. They are part of a movement that is reshaping our economy, and that I believe has the potential to change for the better our country and our world.

Let me tell you why.

Introduction

A LAND OF SCARCITY

IN SEPTEMBER 1991, after travelling through India for the better part of a year, I returned to McGill University to start a Master's in English Literature. I'd been to McGill for my undergraduate degree, but those days were marked as much by the parties and concerts as they were by the last-minute essay writing; in short, a not atypical undergraduate experience. But after working in the teeming streets of Calcutta and studying music in the holy city of Benares, I had a new appreciation for the remarkable opportunity afforded by an institution like McGill. So I returned with a renewed industriousness and a heightened interest in learning.

This new focus brought with it a new awareness of the rich architectural, linguistic, political, and historical experience that comes with a storied city like Montreal. I came alive to the details of the world around me, and I tried to understand for the first time the issues that animated the city's political life. I also became fascinated by the layered history of my surroundings, which was always present but not always immediately apparent.

The city told stories about the past. Walking through the streets of the Old Port or hiking up the mountain in the shadow of the Cross — and even, of course, the name of McGill University itself — was an echo of days gone by, when Montreal was a bustling entrepreneurial hub of 10,000 tucked along the shores of the St. Lawrence River.

I recall stopping one day to take a look at a statue along the main road that leads through the centre of campus. I had passed it countless times, walking along the leafy street, without even so much as noticing it. The work depicts the university's founder, James McGill, walking briskly and holding with one hand a cane while the other is placing his hat on his head. The statue has an aura of enterprise about it, the busy man on the go, bursting with ambition. It was, more than I knew at the time, this ambition that had built not only a university, but also a city and a country.

But while McGill University is the most prominent testament to its founder, another local Montreal institution tells the true story of James McGill and his compatriots. I stumbled upon it one day when I walked into the Fairmount Queen Elizabeth Hotel, an historic site whose famous guests have included Fidel Castro, Nelson Mandela, and the Dalai Lama. It also became the centre of the world's attention in 1969, when John Lennon and Yoko Ono staged their "bed-in" for peace.

I was thinking about all of this as I was walking through the hotel's foyer toward its distinguished five-star eatery, the Beaver Club. Near the restaurant's entrance was a bronze logo with the image of a beaver felling a tree and the words "Industry and Perseverance" printed on a banner. Across the top of the logo were the words "Beaver Club Instituted Montreal," and across the bottom was the date, "1785." Though today the Beaver Club is only a restaurant, it was once the true beating heart of a commercial enterprise that defined our country like no other.

It was past midnight, and the assorted collection of gentlemen were seated on the floor of the hall, singing rowdy French songs as they made paddling motions as if on an imaginary voyage by canoe. Liquor flowed copiously into their mugs and sloshed onto the ground, where it lubricated the floor. Some of the men had already passed out; broken glass and china was scattered across the floor and the wooden table where, only recently, they had enjoyed a meal of flaming boar's head, braised venison, partridge, quail, wild rice, and, of course, a great variety of alcohol.

Looking around, one could see some of the most distinguished men of the era (though you might have been excused for not recognizing them as such at this particular moment). James McGill — fur trader, politician, philanthropist, and one of the richest men in Montreal — was there. You might spy as well the explorer Alexander Mackenzie, whose many accomplishments included being the first European to travel by land to the Pacific Ocean. Or Simon Fraser, who had followed the footsteps of Mackenzie along the raging river that today bears his name, making his way to Vancouver. Another explorer, Joseph Frobisher, was likely there too; he and his brother Thomas had been the first to travel to Churchill River. Frobisher also bore another distinction; he was a founder of the North West Company, and so responsible for this strange, ritualistic society known as the Beaver Club. Almost everyone in attendance was connected in some way to the company; William McGillivray, Alexander Henry, Isaac Todd, they were all there.

Actually, they had little choice. The rules of the club were clear: any member who was in town at the time of a meeting was obliged to attend "except prevented by indisposition." [1]

Becoming a member, though, was not so easy. One had to have wintered in the *pays d'en haut*, the desolate land above Lake Superior where the North West Company plied their trade in beaver pelts. The rules were so strict, in fact, that the original founder of the company, the Scottish entrepreneur Simon McTavish — dubbed "le Seigneur" in the Montreal community — was not allowed entry at first, because although he had been to Lake Superior, he had never wintered over. It wasn't until 1792 that he was finally allowed in the club.

The dinners started early, at 4 p.m., and ended with the last man standing. In between, they participated in a series of rituals that celebrated the rough life of the *coureurs du bois*. Early on in the evening, they raised the same five toasts: To the fur trade in all its branches; To the mother of all saints; To the King; To voyageurs, wives, and children; To absent members. The evening progressed to an extravagant feast, drinking, dancing (often on the table), more drinking, singing, and toward the end of the evening the re-enactment of "le grand

---

1   Notes from the actual meetings were rarely taken, so this account is a dramatization. The members, however, and their rituals, are known to us. In this respect, then, the account is based on historical facts.

voyage," a simulated canoe ride, in which all the members would sit on the floor as if in a canoe and pretend to paddle.

On that particular night, there might have been any number of other invited guests. Many notable people had made appearances over the years. General Isaac Brock, who was to achieve fame for his defence of Upper Canada in the War of 1812 and his eventual death at the Battle of Queenston Heights, had been in attendance at least once. General Roger Hale Sheaffe, who would take command of the British forces when Brock fell, had also made an appearance. But on this occasion, the outsider who garnered the most attention — a most unlikely guest indeed — was Lord Selkirk, the controlling shareholder of the Nor'westers' hated archrival: the Hudson's Bay Company. In fact, the North West Company had been established primarily to break the monopoly of the Hudson's Bay Company, which used its control over vast territories and their access to shipping routes through Hudson's Bay to dominate the lucrative fur trade.

Under control from London, the Hudson's Bay owners profited handsomely from their unique disposition from the British Crown. By contrast, the Nor'westers (as the North West Company principals and employees were called) were a rough and ragged group of largely Scottish entrepreneurs whose raison d'être was best expressed by the Beaver Club motto: "Fortitude in Distress." Many of them had been to the *pays d'en haut* themselves, and took pride in knowing their way through the unforgiving wilderness. They were, by and large, rough-and-ready explorers-cum-entrepreneurs, the "rampaging free enterprisers of the North American frontier."

The North West Company had come out of nowhere and quickly dominated most of the trade in animal pelts. By the early part of the nineteenth century, scarcely two decades after their founding in 1779, they controlled 78 percent of the Canadian fur industry, selling more than 100,000 beaver skins in a typical year, along with almost as many skins of other valuable animals, including bear, fox, marten, mink, lynx, wolf, and otter. Although the Hudson's Bay Company enjoyed distinct advantages — in particular, the cost of shipping beaver pelts by boat through Hudson Bay was significantly cheaper and more efficient than humping them by canoe across the wide countryside, through the Great Lakes, and up the St. Lawrence River — the Nor'westers enjoyed a character advantage.

Classic entrepreneurs, they travelled farther, worked harder, and were willing to suffer hardships and take risks that their competition was not. They enjoyed their image as the rough-and-ready adventurers, and it had given them an edge in a competitive commercial environment. They had a further advantage in that they were allied closely with the Métis, the descendants of mixed marriages between French voyageurs and Native women. The Métis were openly hostile to the autocratic men of the Hudson's Bay Company, who lacked understanding of the Métis way of life. This alliance with the people who lived their lives in the wilderness, and whose labour helped procure many of the valuable skins, was to give the Nor'westers an extra edge.

And so the North West Company enjoyed a distinct advantage by competing against men who lived a thousand miles away and who had never actually visited the wilderness from which they derived such handsome financial returns. It wasn't until Lord Selkirk used his shares in Hudson's Bay to win a grant of 300,000 acres of land near Winnipeg, and move large numbers of immigrants from his Scottish ancestral home, that the Hudson's Bay Company gained a permanent foothold in Canada.

Today, the Beaver Club is only an ancient echo from the prehistory of our nation. But we can still trace our connections back to that time and that place. Imagine all of these men in the same room together: Mackenzie, Fraser, McTavish, McGillivray, McGill. Their names still resonate, two hundred years later, from one end of the country to the other. Even today, we derive benefits from these early entrepreneurs, who took enormous risks, amassed amazing fortunes, and built the lasting institutions of our country.

The Beaver Club mixed all the elements of the new land — the French, English, Scottish, and Native heritage; a love of the outdoors; and a love of commerce that was to define Canada more than any other enterprise before or since. The combination of toughness, cleverness, ingenuity, and perseverance that is exemplified in the lowly beaver was of course a perfect symbol for the upstart North West Company. For the beaver is a builder unlike any other animal; using trees to dam watersheds, it changes its environment to serve its own needs. For all of these reasons the beaver came to represent the new country that these men were building.

The Nor'westers were to leave a lasting mark on the country. Even after their merger with Hudson's Bay in 1821, echoes of the company still resonated throughout the nineteenth and twentieth centuries as they had established an economic model that would mark the development of the country thereafter. As the first large, homegrown Canadian resource company, it established a blueprint for an economy that grew rich selling its plentiful natural resources to the world.

The canoe routes that were the arteries for the Nor'westers' enterprise would also shape the next great

Canadian industry — lumber — by providing the transportation system for the logs to reach their markets. Eventually water-based transportation gave way to an even more efficient system: the railways. Throughout most of the twentieth century the Canadian Pacific Railway (CPR) and Canadian National (CN) transported our natural resource cargo to commercial markets. The railway helped establish a new era of industry, and is closely tied to the development of the mining industry, one of the country's most important sectors.

But the heritage of the Nor'westers also has a darker side, and that's the story of the depletion of natural resources. The primary reason why the Nor'westers travelled so far from their base in Montreal was because the local beaver populations were declining on account of the fur trade. So merchants had to move farther into the wilderness in order to satisfy the growing demand for pelts. The beaver trade, then, was the first clear example of an industry depleting the resource upon which it relies.

Throughout the nineteenth and twentieth centuries the story was told again and again. Natural resources continued to be the bedrock of the Canadian economy, generating millions of jobs in industries such as pulp and paper, fisheries, hydro, mining, and energy. But like the beaver trade, these resources, which once seemed infinite, eventually pushed up against limits.

The extirpation of the buffalo, the decline of the Eastern cod, and the logging of the vast majority of virgin forests stand as three of many examples.

Eventually governments put in place environmental legislation to try to guard against depleting these natural resources, and they have at times helped to impose limits on resource industries and caused them to work within ecological boundaries. But even that system has proved imperfect, as in many cases governments have failed to act soon enough.

The propensity for modern industry to deplete natural resources was accelerated with the advent of industrialization and globalization. Now ever larger global markets were open to Canadian resource companies, and technology allowed for a much higher rate of resource depletion. Take the fisheries as an example. For centuries, European fishermen had been visiting the Grand Banks in droves in order to satisfy their local markets. But by the mid-twentieth century, an international industry had developed. Fishing fleets from all over the world descended upon Canadian waters, and the ships themselves had changed. Simple sailing vessels had been replaced by enormous fish factories complete with sonar technology and winch-operated nets capable of pulling in hundreds of tonnes of fish at one go. This overfishing led to a peak catch of 810,000 tonnes of Atlantic cod in 1968.

Another example of the negative effects of globalization and technology on our resources is the oil sands. For centuries the oil sands remained untapped, until a combination of global demand (driven in part by a concern for the security of supply in other parts of the world) and new technology development allowed for the extraction of this resource for the first time. Thus the potential to deplete natural resources and create unprecedented environmental damage has massively accelerated since the time of the Nor'westers.

American scientist and evolutionary biologist Jared Diamond's seminal book *Collapse* details a number of societies that failed in part because they depleted natural resources like trees and soil, upon which they were reliant. As a result, they undermined the ecological conditions required for their own survival, helped along in many cases by cyclical climate changes, until they eventually were so weakened that they collapsed.

Diamond's book is a cautionary tale for any society that has failed to value the environmental factors that make civilization viable. He spends much of the book grappling with how human societies make such terrible decisions and act so contrary to their own interests. The answer, according to Diamond, relates to what he calls "rational bad behaviour," a phenomenon that results from a series of perverse incentives in the economic system that cause individuals to act in ways that are contrary to the interests of the group.

Diamond is not the first writer to notice the peculiar tendency of many societies to systematically degrade their environment. In 1833, a professor of political economy at Oxford University named William Forster Lloyd published a book entitled *Two Lectures on the Checks to Population*. In this short work, Lloyd noted that when people were allowed indiscriminate use of common property, they tended to overuse it and degrade it, thus leading to general impoverishment. Lloyd's theory was a direct challenge to political philosopher and economist Adam Smith's concept of the Invisible Hand, which held that in a free market economy each person — working for his or her own benefit — inevitably promotes the common good.

Lloyd's theory would not achieve wide circulation until it was later popularized by ecologist and writer Garrett Hardin, who coined the term "the Tragedy of the Commons" for the title of an article he published in *Science* magazine in 1968. Hardin's article is still a vivid warning about a fundamental structural problem inherent in our economic system. According to Hardin, "Each man is locked into a system that compels him to increase his herd without limit — in a world that is limited. Ruin is the destination toward which all men rush, each pursuing his own best interest in a society that believes in the freedom of the commons. Freedom in a commons brings ruin to all."

Writers such as Diamond and Hardin have helped reframe the issue of sustainability not as a question of morality, but as an issue of economic structures and systems that drive people's actions. They have helped us to understand that until we fully grapple with the economic incentives that drive individuals to behave unsustainably, we will struggle to build a society that is not constantly at risk of the Tragedy of the Commons.

The realization that some environmental problems are caused by a design flaw in the economy is leading to a transformation in the way we approach problems like climate change. The good news is that a variety of tools have the potential to remedy these perverse incentives. In the language of economists, these tools have the effect of "internalizing" costs that had hitherto not been factored into market prices. By internalizing the cost, we can harness the full creative potential of the market to focus on minimizing environmental impacts.

The vehicle for this creativity is the entrepreneur. The entrepreneur is able to identify economic potential and opportunity, and rapidly mobilize labour and capital to develop products that consider these new market dynamics. Through the energy of the entrepreneur, free market capitalism is fundamentally efficient and capable of remarkable innovation. But this is true only if the right market signals are provided.

THE NOTION THAT ENVIRONMENTAL policies may actually have an economic benefit was famously advanced by American economist Michael Porter in what is now referred to as the "Porter hypothesis." Porter held that companies and economies often benefit economically from environmental regulation. He argued that well-designed environmental regulation led to "innovation offsets" that compensated for the costs of complying and in fact resulted in new innovation, which led in turn to dramatic leaps forward in productivity, efficiency, and profitability.

Porter's thesis ran contrary to the accepted wisdom at the time. Yet shortly after his paper was published, a number of countries began to experiment with environmental regulation by using the market economy to drive environmental progress, and vice versa. Twenty years later, we can see the effects of these experiments.

In 1991, Sweden was one of the first countries in the world to implement a carbon tax. Since the revenues of the carbon tax were used to reduce income tax, no additional monies were extracted from the economy. The tax burden was then shifted away from areas that were economically productive (income) and placed on others that were not generally productive (greenhouse gas emissions). Between 1990 and 2006, Sweden's economy grew by 44 percent, while its carbon emissions shrank by 9 percent. Today the country is reaping the benefits of its leadership, boasting a healthy clean-tech sector made up of 3,500 companies with combined revenues of more than US$14 billion.

Not long after Sweden implemented its groundbreaking carbon tax, many other European countries implemented similar programs, including Denmark, Germany, Finland, and the Netherlands. In most cases, increased energy costs as a result of carbon taxes or other environmental taxes had a double dividend of both reducing emissions and benefitting the economy. These findings are largely echoed in the report of the Competitiveness Effects of Environmental Tax Reforms (COMETR) project. The report, prepared for the European Union and co-authored by a consortium of leading researchers, verifies the "double dividend" of reduced emissions and increased growth in countries that have instituted environmental pricing. As a result of these kinds of taxation reforms, Europe today is significantly more energy efficient than North America, requiring half as much energy to generate a unit of economic output as Canada.

Putting a price to carbon is just one example of using the market to drive environmental progress. But there are other strategies, too. Countries such as Denmark and Germany have implemented powerful feed-in tariffs to encourage the production of green energy, including solar and wind. The economic benefits are hard to dispute. Germany has half of the world's solar photovoltaic installations, despite the fact that the country receives only 1,500 hours of sunlight annually, or half that of San Diego. As a result of its strong solar market, the country has attracted more than 250,000 jobs in renewables, and more than 40,000 of those are in solar alone. Similarly, Denmark has become a leader in the growing global wind-power industry, with local companies such as Vestas — the world's largest manufacturer of wind turbines — responsible for providing more than 23,000 jobs.

And while Germany and Denmark are the clearest examples of countries that have driven substantial growth in renewable energy, Japan is a poster child for the viability of energy efficiency. The country has reduced oil imports from 5 million barrels a day in 1973 to 4.12 barrels in 2007, and the economy has doubled in size in that time. Japan's consumption of oil per unit of GDP has dropped by two-thirds since 1973, resulting in savings that Morgan Stanley's Robert Feldman calculates at about $140 billion a year. Japan has also seen a 30 percent increase in fuel-efficient cars, and today low-emissions vehicles account for 21 percent of all cars on the road. It does not seem accidental, then, that Toyota and Honda, both Japanese automakers, have dominated the low-emissions car market and crushed the slower-moving U.S. automakers as the cost of fuel increases.

In each of these cases, it is clear that in the green economy, jobs follow markets. These countries built the conditions to create domestic markets in renewable energy and energy efficiency. Local entrepreneurs were then able to attract capital, thus giving rise to local manufacturers who over time became so sophisticated that they could look beyond their borders and sell into international markets. So the need to develop a green economy is equally about participating in a new era of global commerce and about being good environmental stewards.

Canada has an overwhelming economic interest in managing its natural heritage. A new generation of Canadian entrepreneurs is already building the foundation of a new economy, one that will be defined around resource scarcity instead of resource abundance. Driven by curiosity, adventure, and of course the desire for financial returns — the same incentives that drove the Nor'westers through the *pays d'en haut* — they are articulating a profound insight: that if our economic past was based on depleting natural capital, our future wealth will be based on preserving it.

In the following pages I will tell the story of a number of people who are applying this insight to many of the most important industries in the country — forestry, water, electricity, cars, fossil fuels, and agriculture — and in the process building a new economic model for the future.

Chapter One

IF A TREE FALLS

IN THE SUMMER OF 1987, I took a plane from Montreal to Vancouver and then on to Prince George with a couple of university buddies. Our destination was Burns Lake, also known as the "Gateway to Tweedsmuir Park" — a small lumber town, population 2,000, smack in the middle of the province of British Columbia. We drove through the beautiful B.C. interior, past stunning lakes, through the meandering hills and forests, until we pulled into the driveway of George and Bernice Magee.

Uncle George, my mother's brother, had moved to Burns Lake when he finished medical school in the 1960s. There he built a successful medical practice, and with his wife Bernice raised three kids on a large property that doubled as a ranch, complete with horses and stables. I'd come out there before, when I was a boy, with my father. I remember riding horses with George and his kids through these rough hills, always on the lookout for a grizzly bear. The wild, expansive landscape made southern Ontario seem tame by comparison.

This time I was visiting for a different reason. My buddies and I thought George and Bernie's car, a circa-1970 lime green 3/4-ton Suburban, would be the perfect vehicle for six university students who were planting trees for the summer. They had agreed to sell it to us, but the deal was, if we returned it in close to the same shape at the end of the summer, they would buy it back.

It seemed like a perfect arrangement, and the next day we headed back out on the highway, that old Suburban lumbering like a bull moose toward our campsite. I can't remember exactly where that site was, but I do remember careening over mountainous roads as we drove into the night, Neil Young's jangly guitar and voice drifting plaintively from the tape deck: *"Ton-i-i-i-ght's the N-i-i-i-ght."* We arrived well past midnight in a remote campsite in the middle of nowhere, pulled over when we saw the other trucks, pitched our tents in the dark, and climbed into our sleeping bags for a very short sleep.

We were rudely awakened just past 5 a.m. by the sounds of stirring all around us. I poked my head wearily from the tent and was alarmed to see a small army of dirty tree planters stumbling like zombies through the early morning light toward the cook tent. Equally startling was the terrain: an endless moonscape of burnt stumps of trees, and nothing green in sight. This was our new home.

That first day was an experience that thousands of my Canadian compatriots will likely recall as I do: a living out of the parable of Sisyphus. Each tree seemed to be a battle to plant, as we dove through brambly scrub, seeking soil in beds of rock, all the while being harassed by bugs that in both number and size were on a whole different scale than anything I'd experienced before. The heat, the dirt, the sheer boredom forced me to ask a fundamental question: how long can I last at this? The only thing holding me back from quitting on that first day was my pride. I would never recover it if I stormed off so soon; otherwise, I would have been walking back along that dirt road toward Prince George.

It didn't help that by the time the foreman called us in for dinner, easily twelve hours after we started, we were lucky if we'd cleared two dollars an hour after paying for our camp costs. How was one to make a go of this? How was I going to wake up and do this one more day, let alone one week, one month — much less the two months that we'd signed up for?

And yet, after dinner, after a swim in a freezing mountain river, after a cold beer left in said river, and after warming up by the camp fire, I was revived enough to say, let's give it another day. And that second day was a little less brutal, I made a little more money, and soon enough I was getting the hang of it. I lasted three summers.

I've come to see those days as some of the best of my life. The physical labour was purifying. Being outside, working hard in the woods to make some money: it was an education for the soul. At night we'd light a fire, bring out a case of beer, and strum our guitars. In short, it was a pretty good way to spend a few summers. But as time has gone on, I've also come to see other virtues in my tree-planting career. After I left university and started a magazine, I often thought of the trees I had planted, and how in some way perhaps they compensated for the paper used to print the magazine. I figure over those three summers I may have planted somewhere in the range of 250,000 trees, and assuming that they were still growing and healthy, that would take care of quite a lot of years of magazine publishing. It pleased me to know that in some great universal equation I could say that my contribution to the earth perhaps equalled what I had consumed.

Later, of course, when climate change and the role that forests play in taking carbon dioxide out of the atmosphere became more topical, those 250,000 trees made me feel even more virtuous. If they have grown, they would go a long way toward neutralizing my carbon footprint (and those of this book, too). My great environ-mental judge in the sky (my guilty conscience) would be even more pleased.

Or so I thought until I recently returned to Burns Lake and the B.C. interior.

THE FLIGHT FROM VANCOUVER to Smithers is perhaps one of the most beautiful I have ever been on. It is the summer of 2006, and my colleagues and I are going to see a reservoir in central B.C. where Triton Logging — the world's leading company in cutting submerged forests — is harvesting fibre. The first fifteen minutes after takeoff you pass over the Georgia Strait, a vast panorama of blue ocean dotted with mountainous islands that are covered in thick, verdant ancient forests — forests that even from the plane look large and imposing. You can also see the whitecaps of the waves that roll across from Vancouver Island, tiny white tears in a pristine blue canvas.

Eventually, the plane turns inland and heads over the Coastal Range of the Rocky Mountains, where even in summer the glaciers still flow down endless rocky tracts. Mountain lakes and rivers shimmer with an almost unnatural aqua-green colour. Soon, as you pass over the peaks, the infinite forests of British Columbia appear — mile after mile of uninterrupted trees and only a few tiny settlements in sight.

But against this backdrop of visual perfection, you can't help but notice the unusual colour of the forest. Instead of the deep, rich green that one would expect, a distinct rusty-red hue can be seen from the plane. In some places it merges into a grey-brown; it looks as if the forests have been consumed by drought or perhaps fire.

"That's the pine beetle," Triton Logging's founder, Chris Godsall, explains to me as I look out the window.

And I realize, as I look down over places I had been years earlier as a young tree planter, that much of my labour from years gone by was for naught.

THE FORESTS OF BRITISH COLUMBIA are dying. Or, more precisely, the lodgepole pine forests are dying from what many are calling the first large-scale blight caused by global warming. The culprit is the mountain pine beetle, an age-old denizen of the B.C. forests that has been turned into a super-pest due to rising temperatures, and as a result has put one of our country's greatest resources at risk.

The mountain pine beetle is no larger than a grain of rice, and yet it is able to kill an organism millions of times its size with ease. Females fly to a new lodgepole pine tree, burrowing into the bark to lay eggs. As they do so, they release a pheromone that attracts more beetles to the tree. The battle is joined, but not over. The tree has defences; it releases a toxic resin that can kill the beetles. But the bugs have even more weaponry: they carry spores of a fungus, which infect the tree beneath the bark and provide food for the new larvae. Eventually the tree succumbs to disease. Within a few months the needles become a light yellow. They will turn red within a year. This is the colour I saw, the light red tint of the dead and dying needles. Soon thereafter the needles will fall off the tree, and the forest will appear grey.

While the pine beetle has forever been a feature of British Columbia's forests, its populations have previously been held in check by the cold winters. A temperature of −40°C in winter, or −20°C in late spring or early fall, is cold enough to kill the larvae. In the past these conditions happened regularly in the B.C. interior, but not anymore; the province has warmed an average of 4°C in the last ten years, and as a result the mountain pine beetle's numbers have multiplied exponentially in the normally inhospitable forests. When their numbers were less numerous they infected only old or sick trees, playing a natural role in culling the forests and allowing room for new growth. Today, their greater numbers are putting even healthy trees at risk. Add to this the fact that our forests, thanks to tree planters such as myself, are increasingly monocultures and therefore much more susceptible to an epidemic of this sort. The result today can be seen in endless miles of dead forest.

The pine beetle epidemic has had ripple effects. The dense coat of needles that fall from dead or dying trees disrupts the regeneration process; cones that fall to the forest floor have a much more difficult time penetrating the needles and germinating. As a result, these dead forests take longer to regenerate, even more so than a forest affected by fire. In short, as is so often the case in nature, a shift in the natural cycle of just one forest produces a myriad of secondary effects that in the end affects the entire ecosystem.

But the pine beetle is not only affecting the environment; the epidemic is having a major impact on the economy, too. Since 1840, commercial logging has been a mainstay of British Columbia's economy, accounting for more than $17 billion in annual revenue and 84,000 jobs. Ironically, the pine beetle epidemic has created a mini-boom, as forestry companies rush to take down the trees while the lumber is still good. A sort of manic industriousness has come over central B.C. The roads are clogged with logging trucks, the mills are working to capacity, and everyone is being paid handsomely to disassemble a dead forest.

But the end of this logging boom is in sight. The trees are already losing value, as moisture loss causes the wood to shrink and split. And the drier, more brittle wood requires more energy to mill on account of the additional friction caused by lack of moisture in the fibres. Furthermore, the distinct blue stain that the beetles leave behind when they burrow through the tree makes the wood undesirable for many markets. The Japanese market, for example, does not welcome beetle-infected wood, and considers the discolouration a sign of decay.

So a lot of people are starting to wonder what will happen when the pine forests have been logged, or when time runs out and the wood becomes unmarketable. As chance would have it, one of those people is Bernice Magee, the aunt who sold me the lime green Suburban twenty years ago. After her kids grew up and moved out, Bernie launched a new career in politics that landed her the mayoralty of Burns Lake just when the beetle population was beginning to explode. She has since become a world beetle expert, since Burns Lake is effectively ground zero for the mountain lodgepole pine beetle epidemic.

According to Bernie, 80 percent of the forests around Burns Lake are lodgepole pine, and she guesses that 85 percent of that forest has been affected. For a community whose largest employer is the pulp and paper mill, that's huge. So Bernie now spends her days thinking about how the community will respond to these changes, and lately she's been wondering if there was anything they could have done to stop it.

As Bernie remembers it, in the mid-1990s residents did notice an increased prevalence of pine beetle in Tweedsmuir Park, a 981,000-hectare provincial park that is nestled between the Ootsa–Whitesail Lakes, the Coast Mountains, and the Interior Plateau. Local residents recommended that the government oversee a controlled burn of the forests to help stem the beetle population. But the government left the problem to nature to sort out. After all, nature had dealt with these issues in the past, and it was not illogical to assume that it would do so again. What they didn't know then, but what everyone knows for certain now, is the connection between climate change and the beetle epidemic. According to Bernie, this connection is not disputed in the area. The warming temperatures are clearly linked to the explosion of the beetle population, according to residents of all political persuasions and sympathies.

The potential impact on the province — let alone

the immediate community — is staggering. By 2006, 9.2 million hectares of forest were affected, which accounts for more than 12 million cubic metres of trees. Since then this number has only grown. The province estimates that by 2013, more than 80 percent of the merchantable lodgepole pine, which makes up more than half of the timber harvests in the province, will be dead in the central and southern interior. In addition, a report by the Business Council of British Columbia predicts a decline of between 20 and 40 percent of B.C.'s interior forest industry after the dead trees have been cut. In a province where the forest industry is responsible for as much as 32 percent of the economic base and contributes $1.9 billion annually to provincial and municipal coffers, this loss will have a huge impact on the province's economy. And though the federal government has pledged $240 million to its mountain pine beetle program, this subsidy will hardly compensate for the financial pain that likely will result.

And it may not be only British Columbia that gets hurt. One of the great fears about the pine beetle epidemic is that it will spread east across the country. The beetles have already made the jump across the Rocky Mountains to Western Alberta, and even into lodgepole pine stands in Saskatchewan. Clouds of beetles can be carried on strong winds for hundreds of kilometres, spreading the infestation in ways that are hard to predict or to limit. In 2006 the *State of Canada's Forests* report found that "[t]he epidemic is now threatening different pine species, including the jack pine of the northern boreal forest." Thus the fear that the beetle will not only vault geographical divides, but species divides, is not an unreasonable concern.

In British Columbia the infestation has been limited mainly to lodgepole pine, but as it happens Alberta is the only place in North America where the eastern jack pine and the western lodgepole pine have interbred and hybridized. This hybrid pine tree offers a perfect means for the mountain pine beetle to go east. There is also good evidence that the beetle has mutated and evolved, and is now able to feed on spruce trees.

All of these factors raise fears that the beetle could infiltrate the vast boreal forest that runs all the way across Canada from northern Alberta right through to the Maritimes. If this were to happen, the implications — worldwide, and not just in Canada — could be vast. Canada's boreal forest contains 25 percent of the remaining forest cover in the world, and stores more carbon than any other terrestrial ecosystem. If this system becomes threatened, significant quantities of carbon could be released into the atmosphere, further accelerating global climate change.

All of this, of course, comes at a terribly difficult time for the forest products industry, which continues to face a myriad of challenges. In recent years, the Canada–U.S. softwood lumber disputes led to tariffs on Canadian wood entering the United States. In addition, the collapse of the U.S. housing market in 2008 has led to a steep downturn in export revenues. In the last few years, two hundred mills have slowed production or shut down due to sharp decreases in demand and increased competition from other parts of the world. With three hundred communities across Canada at least 50 percent reliant on forestry, this decline in the industry has had devastating effects on many parts of the country. In short, this industry, which was a bulwark for so many communities for so many years, is today desperate for new ideas to survive and thrive.

WHILE THE B.C. INTERIOR has seen an unprecedented destruction of its forests, there is still a lumber resource whose estimated value is at more than $1 billion. But it's hidden in a most unlikely place: under the waters of Ootsa Lake.

The history of Ootsa Lake is a history of duelling interests of natural resources in Canada and around the world. Until the mid-twentieth century, the area was a series of small lakes connected by the Nechako River, which runs into the Fraser River. But in 1952, the Kenney Dam was erected to create one enormous reservoir approximately 472 metres in length and 97 metres in height, raising the waters by 90 metres (and in the process displacing many settlements of the local Cheslatta First Nations). The Kenney Dam was constructed to provide electricity to Alcan's aluminum smelting operations in Kitimat, more than 82 kilometres away. At the time, it was the largest earth-filled dam in the world.

In the mid-twentieth century, the value of power generation trumped the value of the trees that stood within the flooded area that was to become Ootsa Lake. When the area was flooded, the forests were never cleared — and thus an estimated $1.2 billion of timber remains submerged there today, perfectly preserved by the water. It is this forgotten resource that has attracted Triton Logging, and now me too.

I'm here to see Triton's logging operation, which is recovering trees from the bottom of Ootsa Lake. Triton is one of the only companies in the world to focus entirely on logging the estimated $50 billion of forests submerged in hydroelectric facilities. Our plane puts down in Smithers, B.C. — a community of 5,000 nestled in Bulkley Valley, approximately 100 kilometres northwest of Burns Lake. From there it's a two-hour drive out to Triton's logging operations on Ootsa Lake. We eventually pull up to the side of the lake and get out. As we're putting on the safety gear and lifejackets, the foreman is keen to get information on his team's progress.

"We're logging a tree every couple of minutes, I'd say," the foreman announces. "We're into a good patch and they're coming up fast."

We climb aboard a small outboard boat to get to the barge.

"You have to know where you're driving," the driver of the boat announces, pointing to places where the treetops are sticking out from water around the shallower sides of the lake. "The treetops can be hazardous."

As I am to learn, safety is a major motivation for underwater logging operations worldwide. There are often accidents when boaters hit the treetops, and sometimes people drown. This hazard is a source of potential liability for the governments and companies that manage the reservoirs, and a major reason why the operators of the reservoirs want to harvest the trees.

We arrive shortly at the barge that Triton has established as the base of their operations, and climb aboard. On deck is a large yellow unmanned submersible (I'm tempted to call it a yellow submarine, but am told this is not technically correct as a submarine carries people) held by a crane. There is another yellow box on the barge — the control room for the submersible — and a cabin for the crew. After I'm introduced to the crew, I get a chance to see how the technology works.

The crane picks up the sub, pivots, and slowly drops it into the lake.

"We try to keep it fairly buoyant," the foreman says. "It makes it easier to navigate."

I climb into the other little cabin and shut the door. A young hipster wearing jeans and a Mountain Equipment Co-op fleece jacket is sitting behind the controls, which is surrounded by computer screens. One is a sonar screen. A circular light sweeps across the monitor and outlines dots of blue and red.

"See those dots," he says, "those are the trees." I notice that the controls look like a cross between an airplane and a video game. "This is how I fly the sub," he says, pushing the levers forward. It's one of the slang expressions of submarines I learn — controlling a submersible is not driving or floating; it's flying.

On the computer screens directly in front of him are two images, one from a camera mounted on the front of the submersible, the other from a camera on its roof. As he flies the sub forward, a murky image appears in the upper screen — a faint, dark vertical line.

"That's one," he says as the line grows bigger until I recognize its shape.

And there it is, like a ghost, a standing tree in a dead forest more than fifty years under water. He moves the sub up close enough to extend two grappling hooks and grab the tree.

"It's a big one," he says enthusiastically, as he thrusts a lever that sends a screw forward and drives an inflatable airbag into the side of the tree.

By pushing a button he causes a pneumatic pump to inflate the bag with air. You can see the it fill up on the screen.

"Ready to cut," he calls into his microphone.

"Ready," says a voice from the control room.

"Now we can chop," he says, as he directs a one-and-a-half-metre saw to meet the tree. Less than five seconds later the tree is cut and floating free, drifting slowly to the surface of the water.

Once they are cut, the trees are lifted to the surface by the airbags. From there they are collected by a small tugboat and dragged to another barge, where a crane picks them up and collects them on a floating dock. They are then tugged to the shore, where they dry and are eventually moved to a local mill. Some of the logs are sold to a local high-end furniture maker, who values the colour of the wood and the marketing advantage it gives him in sales to his U.S. customers. Other customers include Dockside Green — a $400-million,

LEED–certified green building project in Victoria, B.C. And most recently one of the winner's podiums at the 2010 Winter Olympic Games in Vancouver was made with wood cut by Triton on Ootsa Lake.

Triton Logging was founded in 2000 by Chris Godsall, who realized the size and potential of this lost, underwater resource. Godsall knew right away that what was needed to develop this resource was a new kind of machine, custom-built to log under water. The company spent the first two years working to develop such a tool, and in 2002 the beta version of the Sawfish made its maiden dive in Ootsa Lake. The Sawfish cut two trees and then broke. But for Godsall, this was still enough to confirm the machine's potential. In 2004, I went to visit Triton's headquarters outside of Victoria to see this fantastic piece of machinery. By that time the kinks of the Sawfish were being worked out, and it had many hours of operation under its belt.

Over the next couple of years I watched the company make significant progress — fine-tuning the technology, building a team, raising capital. Eventually our company became an investor, and I was invited on the board.[2] Throughout 2005 and 2006 Triton continued

---

2   Triton is only one of the companies mentioned in this book in which I, or my company Investeco Capital Corp., have a direct financial interest. Others include EnerWorks, Lotek Wireless, and Woodland Biofuels.

logging operations on a number of B.C. reservoirs, and then began to focus their efforts on other parts of the world, where the value of the logs is much higher. By November 2009, the company made a major step toward acquiring a concession to a significant reservoir in Ghana through a merger with a company founded by Canada's former prime minister, Joe Clark. Clark Sustainable Resource Developments (CSRD) had secured a licence to extract lumber from Lake Volta, which was flooded in 1964 and contains an estimated $2.8 billion in timber. The company expects to start logging there in 2011.

Triton is a classic entrepreneurial story about the reinvention of an old industry for a new time. While embracing its roots in the logging industry, the company has invented a new way of logging that has no impact on living forests. It's in one sense a continuation of what has come before, and in another sense a total revolution.

Standing on the barge at Ootsa Lake, I had a sense of how entrepreneurs are turning the conventional business world upside down, and inventing new ways of doing things that are often radical departures from the past. But at the same time there is a conscious continuity with what has come before. In a modern business environment — where natural capital and ecosystems have a market value — wood fibre in the future might come from a very different place than it used to. The company purposely keeps the word "logging" in its name, in respect of the history of the industry they operate within.

But there is an irony buried in this history. Though it was an economic imperative that drove the industry and built the demand for forest products, our logging practices show a consistent undervaluing of the services that this resource provides. Flooding forests to create hydroelectric facilities, as happened on Ootsa Lake, is an example of how we have placed perhaps too little value on wood and on our trees. But we are learning slowly that even in a country as large as Canada, our forests and trees must be treated as scarce resources. We are also learning that there may be other benefits that can be derived from forest products, including the value of biodiversity, the value to the atmosphere through carbon dioxide sequestration, and increasingly the value of the energy that can be generated from wood fibre.

I'M STANDING BESIDE A HUGE pile of junk. I've come to a transfer station, which is a fancy way of saying an urban graveyard. If you wonder where your old roof goes after the new one's been installed, it's places like this. But the goal is not to discard the waste and take it to a landfill, but rather to look for what can be reused.

By the front door a dump truck is dropping off a load. Most of the waste that gets brought here comes from construction sites, and a good quantity of it is wood. Securing the wood is the goal of this facility. At first the debris is crudely separated by a grapple into piles with less or more wood content. From there the contents are carried along a conveyor belt where they are picked over by people who separate the wood from the non-wood content. Machines using gravity and magnets help further isolate the wood content. At the end of the process the facility is left with a pile of wood chips. While it doesn't look that special, a pile like this is increasing in value as demand for wood products is going up. What's driving this operation is a growing market for biofuels, which turn wood products into energy.

Although using wood to make energy is not a new idea — it remains the dominant source of energy in much of the world for heating and cooking the idea that it can provide a growing share of energy in the developed world is gaining currency in a time of renewed concern about climate change. Using wood as fuel is one way to potentially reduce greenhouse gas emissions, so long as the overall forest cover remains constant and we don't denude the forests for energy.

Our forests provide ample amounts of waste wood that would otherwise rot and release carbon back into the atmosphere. Using this waste wood to create energy is theoretically carbon neutral. For example, the billions of trees infected by the mountain pine beetle are now likely to degrade and rot, and eventually dry out, creating a forest fire hazard. So there is a growing focus on using these trees for energy production. In fact, BC Hydro has put out a number of RFPs that would turn beetle-infested wood into energy.

The move toward bioenergy is giving the forest industry a new lease on life by creating a whole new business sector and potential revenue stream, one that is likely to increase over time. And if companies such as Vancouver–based Nexterra have their way, the move to bioenergy will also reduce the operating expenses of forest companies and make them more profitable.

Nexterra is the creation of Jonathan Rhone, who founded the company in 2003. Trim and energetic, Rhone has a refreshingly youthful air about him. As former CFO of Dynamotive, a company that uses fast pyrolysis — a process that subjects biomass to temperatures in the range of 400°C without the presence of oxygen in order to create biofuels — Rhone has vast experience in the area of biomass, and has also been through the process of getting a new technology company off the ground at least once already. In addition, Rhone has excellent contacts in the Vancouver business community; he is, for example, on the board of Vancity Capital, the highly successful and unique Vancouver–based financial institution.

When Rhone left Dynamotive to start Nexterra, his first order of business was to develop a gasification process using waste wood to provide thermal heat or electricity. The Nexterra process gasifies what's known as "hog fuel" — a by-product of lumber operations that usually consists of small pieces of bark — in a low-oxygen environment at 815°C. This process creates a synthetic gas made up primarily of carbon monoxide, hydrogen, and methane that can be burnt in a thermal oxidizer. It also has the potential to replace natural gas for engines. What makes the process even more interesting, aside from displacing natural gas or propane, is that it creates significant greenhouse gas emissions credits, which can now be sold into a growing market.

After the company had proven the viability of the technology in a small pilot plant, Rhone turned his attention to the commercial market. He focused first on the forest products sector, an industry that spends an estimated $8 billion a year on natural gas and has lots of waste biomass kicking around. In 2006, Nexterra landed their first commercial contract with Tolko Industries, a B.C.–based forest products company, to build a gasification system for the Heffley Creek plywood mill north of

Kamloops. Not only did Nexterra prove they could build the system, the project ended up saving Tolko $1.5 million annually in fuel costs. As an added bonus, the mill reduced its greenhouse gas emissions by 12,000 tonnes a year.

Since its 2006 launch, Nexterra had successfully branched out beyond the forest products industry into a variety of new sectors. Working with partners such as Johnson Controls, a leader in automotive design and power systems, Nexterra has targeted the university sector, completing a plant at the University of South Carolina. They are also building the first residential application of their gasifiers at Dockside Green, a $600-million, 6-hectare, LEED–platinum development in downtown Victoria that will eventually be home to 2,500 residents. And Nexterra garnered some extra bragging rights when it won a contract with the Oak Ridge National Laboratory (ORNL) in Tennessee, the U.S. Department of Energy's largest science lab and the site of the secret Manhattan Project during the Second World War. To finance the company, Rhone and his partners sold a controlling interest to ARC Financial, a Calgary–based investment corporation with a focus on energy. Nexterra is also partnering with General Electric in an effort to develop the technology that will feed the syngas, or synthetic gas, directly into a GE engine.

As companies like Nexterra succeed in developing biomass as a replacement for fossil fuels, there will almost certainly be a growing demand for biofuel, in particular biofuel made from wood waste. This partly explains why the worldwide wood fuel pellet market is expected to double by 2012. If this happens, the next question is where the biomass will come from.

TODAY THERE ARE SIGNIFICANT SOURCES of biomass available. At least for the moment, British Columbia, on account of the beetle-infected wood, has a significant surplus. And according to the BIOCAP Canada Foundation,[3] Ontario's forests could also support a renewable bioenergy industry "sufficient to support at least 27 percent of the total energy needs of the province."

But for companies that need biomass, it's not a theoretical question of whether this material is available, but a much more practical question of at what price and how close the source. Because of the relatively low energy density of biomass, it is typically uneconomical if the source of the biomass is more than 200 kilometres away, as transportation costs can become prohibitive beyond that distance. So the market for biomass is not a world market, but rather an overlapping set of local markets, each with its own unique sources of supply. Companies that want to generate energy from biomass will

---

3   BIOCAP Canada officially ceased operations on March 31, 2008.

have to secure a long-term source at a reasonable price, and more and more this is what the biomass game will be about.

Companies such as Toronto–based Ecostrat are playing a critical role in the supply chain by helping companies secure reliable supplies of biomass. The creation of entrepreneur Jordan Solomon, Ecostrat has spent ten years developing a database of more than 200,000 biomass suppliers. The company claims to track "more than 96 percent of all point sources of virgin and post-industrial wood in North America" to ensure their customers have access to a stable supply of biomass.

Jordan Solomon is at the centre of a growing new demand for wood. He is a classic entrepreneur, with a contrarian streak and a desire to blaze his own path. You can see from the moment you meet him that the qualities that would make him a bad employee make him a good entrepreneur. His open, easygoing manner masks intense ambition and drive.

Solomon came out of university with a degree in environmental studies, and when he saw a market opportunity in the biomass sector he figured he could do a better job on his own and run the company the way he wanted to. Like all entrepreneurs, he's had to take extraordinary risks. A picture of an ocean liner that Ecostrat commissioned to deliver biomass to a client in

Turkey hangs on a wall in his office in Toronto. It was one of the largest contracts in the company's history. It was also a huge financial gamble, as Solomon had to cover the costs of delivery prior to receiving payment. Luckily, the gamble paid off.

Ecostrat has brought ingenuity to the developing biomass market, not only by helping companies identify reliable sources of the product, but by providing some price certainty. Because demand for wood biomass has been increasing on an annual (and sometimes even monthly) basis, long-term prices have been difficult to establish. The price fluctuation is in part due to the fact that biomass suppliers are reluctant to lock in at today's prices. Even when they are willing to strike a long-term price, the contract is only as good as the supplier. Given the volatility of the wood products industry, a biomass plant may secure a long-term contract only to discover that the supplier has gone out of business.

Working with a large American financial services firm, Solomon is able to ensure a degree of price stability by providing a "Biomass Credit Wrap," which gives projects a guaranteed supply at a fixed price for up to fifteen years. These kinds of innovative financial products will help increase the number of biomass plants in North America by providing long-term contracts that offer some certainty on price and product availability.

But Solomon hasn't stopped there. He is now working on a development that promises to revolutionize the forest products sector. One of the largest potential uses for biomass in the developed world is in coal-fired power plants, which are the single largest source of greenhouse gas emissions and air pollution in North America. Coal plants can generate as much as 15 percent of their power output from biomass without costly retrofits to plant equipment. By burning a mix of 15 percent biomass and 85 percent coal in the same boiler, a process called "direct co-firing," both air pollution and greenhouse gas emissions are significantly reduced.

But even coal plants that co-fire biomass create pollution, so there is pressure to go further still. Some jurisdictions are taking more dramatic action to reduce the impact of coal emissions. In Ontario, the Nanticoke power plant, North America's largest coal power plant, is scheduled to be decommissioned by 2014. The facility is now looking at switching fuels from coal to biomass.

But there are challenges to firing coal plants with biomass, especially once you get beyond the 15 percent range. For example, biomass has higher moisture content than coal, which leads not only to lower energy value but also to difficulty in handling and storage. Large power plants need sufficient storage capacity to ensure that there is a constant supply of fuel. But the properties and moisture content of biomass can change when stored. Microbial activity can lead to heating, and even combustion in extreme cases. Another problem with biomass is transportation. Because the energy density of biomass is only 10 percent of coal's, a great deal more biomass is required to produce the same amount of energy as coal. This poses challenges even in the supply and transportation of this volume. As a result, fluctuations in diesel prices can affect the cost of biomass.

One potential solution is torrefaction, a thermo-chemical process that subjects wood to heat of 200°C to 300°C for an hour without oxygen. The process changes the properties of the wood to increase the energy value by weight and make it more impervious to water, thus improving the durability and uniformity of the resulting "char." In short, torrefied wood works and acts a lot like coal. The hope is that it may be able to supplement coal in coal-fired plants without adding major retrofit costs that come with burning green biomass or wood pellets. Torrefied wood could be a major leap forward, and provide enormous environmental gains, if North America's coal infrastructure could be repurposed to burn biomass.

Ecostrat has been working with a few partners on a process to develop torrefied wood on a commercial scale. And Solomon believes his clients in the power industry will embrace this new technology, which has the potential to move coal-fired power plants in a green direction.

BEHIND THE MOVE TOWARD using biomass as a fuel is the realization of the value that forests provide as a carbon dioxide sink. As long as the overall forest cover remains constant, in theory, the use of biomass from forests to create energy should not increase greenhouse gas emissions, unlike fossil fuels, which truly add to atmospheric carbon. As a result, the use of biofuels for energy production creates carbon offsets within most cap-and-trade programs designed to put a price on greenhouse gas emissions. And increasingly these offsets can be sold into carbon markets.

The advent of a market for carbon offsets is already having a broad impact on many sectors of the Canadian economy, including forest products. While for the past decade large pools of capital have been used to purchase international emissions credits and sell them into European markets, this business is still in its infancy in North America because governments have been slow to implement the rules around cap-and-trade programs. But that is slowly changing. Funds like British Columbia's Pacific Carbon Trust are actively buying credits from the forestry industry, among others. The Pacific Carbon Trust is a Crown corporation that was established under the provincial government's Climate Action Plan, which aims to deliver carbon credits and make the public sector carbon neutral by 2010.

Today, the North American carbon market is beginning to accelerate on the back of two serious regional cap-and-trade programs — the Regional Greenhouse Gas Initiative (RGGI), a system focused on the northeastern United States, and the Western Climate Initiative, which centres on the western United States. Both programs have the participation of a number of Canadian provinces. In addition, the United States under President Barack Obama is keen to develop a national cap-and-trade system. At the time of this writing, the American Clean Energy and Security Act, also known as the Waxman–Markey Bill after its two Democratic authors, is moving through the United States Congress. Most of these programs have created carbon credits from projects such as renewable energy and bio-digestion from agricultural waste.

The European market has also partnered with countries in the developing world under Kyoto's Clean Development Mechanism (CDM) by allowing emissions reductions in countries such as China to be sold back into developed markets. The virtue of the CDM is to allow much lower cost CO_2 reductions, and since all countries share the same atmosphere, a tonne of CO_2 eliminated in China has the same climactic impact as a tonne eliminated in England. Many of China's CDM credits have resulted from the destruction of fluoroform (CHF_3, also known as HFC-23), a by-product of certain refrigerants and a greenhouse gas that is 11,700 times more potent than CO_2. Because of the potency of this greenhouse gas and the relative ease of its destruction, the cost of creating a carbon credit from this method is extremely inexpensive, thus drawing in significant capital.

But perhaps even more significant for Canada's economy is the introduction of forestry-related greenhouse gas reduction credits. In the original Kyoto agreement, Canada argued strongly in favour of counting forests as carbon sinks on account of the potential to sequester carbon in forests. This argument was met with resistance in early negotiations. Planting trees was viewed as a dubious form of carbon sequestration — partly on account of a suspicion that it would take attention away from the arguably more important goal of reducing emissions from industry, and partly because of concerns about the credibility of carbon credits derived from forests, particularly those resulting from tree-planting projects.

Accounting for tree mortality through natural causes such as disease or forest fire is critical for determining whether the CO_2 was truly sequestered or not.

And as I discovered in Burns Lake, a beetle epidemic can wipe out a lot of tree planting. Similarly, the issue of the types of trees that are replanted has also raised concerns. For example, replanting a single species monoculture in the Amazon does not seem like a sustainable carbon storage strategy. Aside from the poorer biodiversity that would result, such a monoculture would be in greater danger of being wiped out by disease, thus releasing the carbon back into the atmosphere.

If reforestation is controversial, the debate surrounding avoided deforestation is even more heated. For avoided deforestation to be truly effective in fighting climate change one would have to know that the forest in question would have been cut down had it not been for the offsets, which of course is difficult to determine. But what is clear is that deforestation is one of the largest contributors to climate change, representing around 20 percent of global emissions.

But reducing emissions from avoided deforestation also has the potential to be very cost-effective. In his groundbreaking study, the most thorough consideration of the future costs of climate change to the world's economy, former World Bank chief economist Sir Nicholas Stern advocated for avoided deforestation, arguing that it was "a highly cost-effective way of reducing greenhouse gas emissions [that] has the potential to offer significant reductions fairly quickly." Observers such as Stern recommend a system that would pay landowners to leave forests intact, as opposed to clearing them for alternative land uses such as farming. Even with prices as low as $5 per tonne for avoided deforestation, such a system could prevent the destruction of large swaths of tropical forests in countries such as Brazil, Indonesia, and the Congo. And if the price for avoided deforestation were higher, the effect would be even greater. By one estimate, at $20 per tonne, reduced emissions from avoided deforestation could effectively reduce overall global greenhouse gas emissions by 7 percent.

It's no surprise, then, that over the last few years much time and effort has been devoted to establishing credit for prevented deforestation, or what is now called Reducing Emissions from Deforestation and Degradation (REDD) at international climate change conferences. Pressure has increased to make REDD projects eligible for carbon credits under the Clean Development Mechanism. Much of this pressure has come from countries such as Indonesia and Brazil, which have large forest cover and high rates of deforestation and thus stand to benefit from these projects. But a growing consensus is emerging that REDD could help to reduce global greenhouse gas emissions.

Another reason why REDD garners such interest from the environmental community is for the significant biodiversity benefit it provides. Avoided deforestation may be the best way to preserve tropical forests worldwide, and to save countless species from extinction. The capital secured from the program may also provide an alternative revenue stream for developing countries to counter the powerful economic pressure to clear forests to grow crops for the world food market. In fact, the carbon market is one of the first examples of a market for "natural capital." For the first time, carbon credits, and especially REDD, may put a value to assets that were formerly left off the balance sheet. So the most far-reaching impact of the carbon market is to establish the principle of natural capital, which is that nature should be given real economic value, even if it cannot be determined with precision.

The implications of this new economic system are potentially vast for Canada. With our tremendous land mass, significant forest cover, and incredible store of natural capital, Canada has a huge self-interest in advocating for a system that will place a value on preserving those assets. The boreal forest alone covers an estimated 0.5 billion hectares, or 58 percent of Canada's land mass. Most of us, huddled along the country's southern border, may not appreciate the scope and size of this forest, but it is a tremendous treasure with significant value. As a carbon sink, it is unparalleled in the world, sequestering an estimated

67 billion tonnes of carbon. In fact, a recent study by the Canadian Boreal Initiative came to the startling conclusion that the non-marketable value of the boreal forest in 2002 was $93.2 billion, twice as much as the marketable services derived from the boreal in activities such as forestry, mining, and oil and gas.

This is a critical insight for any country, but particularly for a country such as Canada, which is blessed with abundant natural resources. Canada's forests already have incredible importance to the world — as a supply of fibre, as a carbon sink, and as a source of biodiversity. The forest industry has been overly focused on the first benefit, and perhaps not enough on the latter two. Looking forward, though, it seems clear that the greatest value will come from having these benefits in balance. The Forest Products Association of Canada has announced plans to be carbon neutral by 2015, and it seems that the industry now agrees.

Finding a market mechanism for protecting the broader value of our natural capital — not just the value of the goods and products that we can extract and sell, but also the value that we derive through other non-commercial uses — is critical to Canada's future prosperity. But REDD programs have not yet been extended to countries such as Canada. And until we reduce our emissions, the world remains reluctant to pay a country to manage its natural capital. However, over time it is possible — perhaps likely — that this market failure will also be remedied, that the huge, untapped wealth of the northern boreal forest will be given a value, and that future entrepreneurs may make their fortune preserving it.

WHEN WE FULLY UNDERSTAND all of the ways that forests interact with other parts of the environment, we may begin to grasp their true value. In British Columbia, the dying lodgepole pine will leave a changed environment. Gone are the root systems that acted like sponges, soaking up excess water. The formerly dry forest floor is now often wet, affecting animals such as caribou, which feed on the dry lichen that is found in pine forests. And with the living root systems gone, the water is running from the forests, thus raising water levels and silting up lakes and rivers. Excess water has led to flooding in places like the Fraser Valley watershed, which contains seven million hectares of pine forest. All of these issues underline the intimate connection between our forests and an equally important resource: water.

Chapter Two

WATER, WATER EVERYWHERE

CONSIDERED BY SOME TO BE A sixth Great Lake, Georgian Bay is a 15,000-square-kilometre body of water separated from Lake Huron by Manitoulin Island, the largest freshwater island in the world. Distinguished by its aqua-coloured water, its smooth rocks, and its many islands — which have earned the moniker "The 30,000 Islands" — Georgian Bay holds a mythical place in the minds of many Canadians, in part because it is the subject of a number of famous Group of Seven paintings. The spare pine trees that distinguish Georgian Bay — bent like hunched-over old men huddling against the prevailing west winds — seem to capture something essential about the spirit of a sparsely populated country that has been shaped by its hard surroundings.

Since I was eight years old I have come here every summer. For many years I went to Hurontario, a summer camp extolling the virtues of canoeing, camping, sailing, and all things "woodsy." Later I became a counsellor, leading canoe trips that wound through the whitewater rivers that empty into Georgian Bay. We would camp out near the shore, and during the day we would set out again on the ocean-sized waves.

When I met my wife, one of the things that we shared was our love of Georgian Bay. Like me, she had spent all her summers here, since the very first month of her life. When we were dating she took me to her island in Pointe au Baril. Four Winds is a desolate out-crop of rock perched at the edge of the open water. The island is 2 hectares of rugged Canadian Shield with a couple of shrubby trees and not much else. Stand-ing on the shores and watching the waves crashing in can make you feel like you are at the very edge of the earth. The island personifies the unique, rugged beauty of this area, a beauty that is spare and simple and primal. Even as life to the south grows more hectic, even as the pleasure boats and speed boats increase in number, this place has retained its wildness, and I hope it always will.

In the 1970s my wife's parents bought their cottage as a summer retreat. Jillson, my mother-in-law, would pick up the kids in a loaded car on the last day of school and they would all head north for the summer. The cottage itself is no more than a simple wood fishing cabin. Magnificently rustic, it is in large part a museum to summers spent in the wilderness: snake skins hang from chandeliers, paper drawings of bass caught in earlier years are pinned to the walls, and camp badges and awards are scattered throughout.

A few things have changed on Four Winds, but not too much. When a whole new generation of kids arrived — seven cousins were born in seven consecutive years — we built a couple of sleeping cabins to accommodate the growing numbers. We pulled down the "shitters" and put up some nice new composting toilets. A solar water pump was installed. But for the most part, it's the same as it ever was: candles are lit at night, there's a propane stove, clothes dry on a line, and we live in tune with nature's rhythms.

Despite our best efforts to keep to tradition, Four Winds is changing because the water is changing. For years, the water levels have been falling, and it is altering the island and the surroundings. You can see it especially in the shoals that surround the island. Ever since I started going to Four Winds I have delighted in paddling out in front of the cottage, where the waves roll in over the rocks and break. But over the last few years, the topography of the land has changed dramatically. Today in many places where I once paddled there are now a string of islands instead. When we walk on them with the kids, I tell them, "I used to canoe right here where we're walking." It's hard to imagine that they were under water fifteen years ago.

There are other changes. The place where my brother and sister-in-law were married is no longer beside the water, but rather 10 metres up on the shore. The pile of rocks is still there, where we stood the podium, but it looks like they've been moved. And the markers we put out to warn boats of shoals are now a metre off the ground. Most noticeably, it's getting harder to dock the boat. Where once there was an easy passage through a wide opening, there is now an extremely narrow channel.

Other neighbouring islands have been even more affected. As you look south you will see Kishkedena, a 4-hectare marvel of bent pines and smoothly curved stone. But getting there can be a problem. In the past twenty years I have watched a regular boat channel narrow to the point of being barely passable. Where you once could have traversed the waters by cruiser, today — unless you know exactly where you are going — you'd be lucky to get by in a small outboard. In some places the channel is no more than 6 metres wide.

Although 2009 offered somewhat of a respite, with water levels increasing for the first time in about ten years, for much of the past decade the water in Georgian Bay and Lake Huron had fallen to historically low levels. And the implications, if the trend continues, could be a lot more serious. Nervous cottagers in the area have established task forces to discuss the problem and how to deal with it. At first many cottagers were convinced that erosion caused by dredging the St. Clair River allowed excess water to drain out of Lake Huron and into Lake Erie like an unplugged bathtub. In 2005, the Georgian Bay Association commissioned a study that supported this hypothesis, but in 2009 a report to the International Joint Commission on the Great Lakes disputed this finding.

But whether or not dredging the St. Clair River is a contributing factor, most agree that the decline in water levels in the Great Lakes is due at least in part to the impact of climate change. Perhaps this is not too surprising, for climate has been largely responsible for the rise and fall of the Great Lakes since the end of the last ice age around 10,000 years ago. Indeed, around 7,900 years ago, the water levels of the Great Lakes fell so dramatically due to a particularly hot and dry climate that rivers that had once flowed out of them evaporated completely. This left the Great Lakes essentially landlocked, or, to use the common scientific terminology, they became "terminal."

A number of scientists are looking now at whether it is possible that, with advanced climate change, those kinds of conditions could be repeated in the next hundred years. According to one study cited by Natural Resources Canada in a report prepared for its Enhancing Resilience in a Changing Climate program, a temperature increase of around 4°C coupled with a 50 percent decrease in precipitation patterns could cause the Great Lakes to once again become terminal. While this scenario is indeed an outlier, most studies suggest a likely drop between 0.23 metres and 2.5 metres in the next hundred years, depending on the effects of climate change.

There are a couple of ways that climate change could be affecting the water levels of the Great Lakes already. Hotter summers lead to greater evaporation and less runoff into the lakes, while warmer winters lead to less ice cover, greater exposure to the sun and wind, and therefore increased evaporation in the winter months. So the Great Lakes are likely losing more water to evaporation than they normally would, a process that would continue or worsen as climate change accelerates.

The idea that a small amount of evaporation could lead to changes in bodies of water of that size defies most people's understanding of how water cycles work. But just as our atmosphere has come to appear a lot more vulnerable to human intervention, so too has our hydrologic cycle. Although the Great Lakes are the largest system of surface freshwater on earth, with more than 22 cubic kilometres of water or over 20 percent of all the surface freshwater in the world, they are still vulnerable to change. Despite their huge size, only 1 percent of the water volume is renewed in any given year. The remaining 99 percent is a remnant of the last ice age, and if lost would not be replenished. So the cumulative effects of these small changes over time can lead to large changes that may not be reversible.

Indeed, the best guess from scientists today is that the water levels of the Great Lakes will decline in the coming decades by around a metre. This of course poses a problem to the hundreds of thousands of cottagers in the area, but even more so the residents who rely on the water for more than just recreation. Because the Great Lakes are home to 25 percent of Canada's population and supports 45 percent of the nation's economy, it won't just be the cottagers who are affected by their fluctuating levels; it could be the entire country. After all, our economy has become heavily reliant on access to water. Take the automotive industry, for example — the historical mainstay of the economy of the Great Lakes basin in recent years (though its hegemony appears to be questionable for the future, as I will discuss in a later chapter); it's estimated that 400,000 litres of water are required to manufacture just one car. So access to water is vital for provinces like Ontario that have a strong manufacturing base.

But it's not only the manufacturing sector that will feel the effects of water scarcity. Almost every major industry from power generation to agriculture is reliant on water, and that reliance has the capacity to affect and alter the delicate balance of our hydrologic cycle. Water levels also affect transportation, and the Great Lakes are a vital shipping corridor. Over the last decade freighters have been forced to reduce their cargo due to shrinking water lanes, thus reducing income on average by $6,000 to $12,000 per trip. And the water supply is vital to our food security. Despite the growing population and urbanization of southern Ontario, the Great Lakes basin still generates 25 percent of Canada's food production.

But if the Great Lakes region is vulnerable to water changes, it pales in comparison to some other parts of the country, particularly Alberta and Saskatchewan, where water is an even more serious ecological and economic issue. It is one of the many ironies that Alberta, the province that has benefitted the most from the use of fossil fuels, may also be hit the hardest by climate change. Even more ironic, perhaps, is that the first hit will be the oil sands projects, one of the single largest contributors to climate change in the country.

Current oil sands projects have reduced the flow of the Athabasca River significantly. In fact, the 359 million cubic metres of water that is consumed annually by the oil sands is already twice what is required by the city of Calgary. And that heavy water use is likely to grow in coming years. Analysts expect that by 2030, withdrawals from the Athabasca River to service the oil sands will increase fivefold. Concern for this incredible appetite for water has led to broad criticism of the oil sands projects from sources as diverse as the World Wildlife Fund and former premier of Alberta Peter Lougheed.

Even without the exorbitant amount of water used by projects such as the oil sands, Alberta and much of Western Canada are particularly vulnerable to climate change, as the warmer temperatures are depleting the glaciers that feed many western rivers. In addition, because of warming temperatures, and hence warmer soil conditions in many rivers, less water is running through the rivers and more is being absorbed into the river floor.

We can already see this effect at play in Western Canada. Water flow in Alberta's rivers declined by 30 percent in the last century, and, according to Environment Canada, glacier-fed rivers in Western Canada — such as the Saskatchewan–Nelson River Basin — are already experiencing a decline in water flow that had not been anticipated by scientists for years to come. This has a wide array of consequences, from decreased hydroelectric power generation to changes in fish habitat and breeding.

But of all the problems associated with water loss, the most alarming may be the potential impact on agriculture, which accounts for around 9 percent of all water withdrawals in Canada. While some climate models suggest a slight increase in agricultural yields in Canada on account of a potentially longer growing season, along with the added benefit of higher levels of atmospheric CO_2, which can increase crop productivity, there is no question that after a certain amount of warming — probably somewhere in the range of 3°C — agricultural production in Canada will fall as higher temperatures lead to greater water scarcity. These negative effects will not be distributed evenly. Some parts of the country may fare well, but other regions will be hit hard as agricultural conditions deteriorate. And again the prairie provinces — the big winners in the energy sweepstakes — look like they might have a losing ticket in the water lottery.

Alberta, which accounts for roughly 60 percent of all irrigated land in Canada, is particularly vulnerable to drought. In the mid-1930s, marginal rainfalls devastated crop yields and led to an estimated 200,000 farm failures and an exodus of 300,000 people. Another drought in 2001 to 2003 saw the province lose more than a billion dollars in revenue. In the spring of 2009, entire crops were wiped out across the prairies. And it is likely that more dry weather is on the way. In fact, a comprehensive published study entitled "An Impending Water Crisis in Canada's Western Prairie Provinces," co-authored by W. F. Donahue and David Schindler of the University of Alberta, anticipates that the effects of climate change will lead to a "crisis in water quantity and quality with far-reaching implications" for the province.

The desperate state of water in Alberta has already given rise to a new market mechanism that allows for trading water quotas. Similar to the way offsets are traded in a carbon market, those who have excess water can sell it to others who are not able to get new licences or have exceeded their licences. This market turns on a recent ruling by Alberta Environment to separate water rights from land rights. The cost of water has climbed precipitously, so much so that the Municipal District of Rocky View agreed to pay $15 million to provide water for a racetrack and shopping centre.

But if Western Canada is already feeling the pain of water scarcity and drought as a result of climate change, parts of the United States are likely to fare even worse. In the southwest, water resources are expected to diminish by up to one-third by mid-century. And as in the Canadian prairies, a combination of declining glacial melts, increased evaporation, and greater water use are leading to drastic declines in freshwater resources in the U.S. Midwest. The effects are already visible. For example, so much water is taken from the Colorado River that at times it cannot reach the ocean; and Lake Mead, part of the Colorado River system and a key source of water for an estimated 8 million people, has a 50 percent possibility of running dry by 2021. Similarly, the Ogallala Aquifer, which stretches from North Dakota to Texas and is a primary source of water for much of the Great Plains, is estimated to have lost 325 billion cubic metres of water, eighteen times the annual volume of the Colorado River. These are only a few examples of a much broader phenomenon that will likely see large tracts of the United States experience serious challenges to supply fresh water to their growing populations.

There is little doubt that climate change is making a bad situation worse. For example, in the last few years, parts of the American Midwest and California have become increasingly vulnerable to forest fire due to long periods of drought. In October 2007, with rainfall patterns in California just one-sixth of their seasonal average, almost a million were forced from their homes as wildfires swept through the state, accelerated by 100 kilometre-per-hour winds.

A natural question, and one that has been hotly debated in recent years, is whether the U.S. will use NAFTA, the WTO, or other means to get access to Canada's plentiful water supplies. Experts are split on the question, and so far a challenge to Canada's sovereignty over its water has never been tested through NAFTA. However, activists such as Maude Barlow of the Council of Canadians warn that a U.S. raid on our water resources is a likely threat. Although some of her predictions sound openly alarmist (a media release issued by the Council of Canadians in May 1998, entitled "National Sovereignty Dripping Away Under NAFTA," quoted Barlow as saying that "unless federal government action is taken very soon, it is almost certain that Canada will be exporting water within the year"), there is no doubt that Canada's ability to exercise sovereignty over water resources strikes a deep chord with its citizens. According to a poll by Environics, 88 percent of Canadians are fearful of bulk exports of water to the U.S. and are suspicious that trade agreements may put our water resources at risk. This fear is shared by many mainstream Canadian pundits and commentators. In fact, former Alberta premier Peter Lougheed gave credibility to the cause when in 2007 he predicted that "the United States will be coming after our water in three to five years."

The pressure may not come from outside our borders, but rather from within. The Montreal Economic Institute, a blue-chip Quebec–based think tank, called for Canada to consider large-scale water exports as a "wealth-creating idea for Quebec and for Canada as a whole," which they claimed could bring in $65 billion a year in revenue. If their numbers are correct, such a trade agreement may be difficult to resist. Although the federal government has twice rescinded permits to export bulk water sales to the U.S., there is a risk that one day they may turn a blind eye.

Though the pressures from within North America over scarce water resources will be significant, they are likely to pale in comparison to those in other parts of the world. Scientists at the Institute for Environment and Human Security (UNU-EHS), a group from Bonn, Germany, that is affiliated with the United Nations, estimate there will be as many as 50 million environmental refugees by 2050, and 200 million by 2080, mostly due to changes in water distribution as a result of climate change. Whole regions such as sub-Saharan Africa are expected to see crop yields decline by between 5 and 10 percent by 2050, on account of decreased rainfall and increased droughts. In places such as Bangladesh, where monsoon flooding is already a problem for millions, it's likely to be too much water that's the problem. The moral, financial, and perhaps one day legal responsibility for these growing populations will rest principally with rich Western countries that are the major contributors to climate change and that have the financial resources to help deal with it.

The impending challenges around water use in the twenty-first century are shining a new spotlight on the economics of water. The Tragedy of the Commons is more apparent in our use of water than in our use of virtually any other resource, for the principal reason that it is either free or extremely cheap. There is growing evidence that these low water prices encourage wastefulness. In a recent study on water use commissioned by the Organisation for Economic Co-operation and Development (OECD), Canada ranked a dismal twenty-eighth (just above the United States) of the twenty-nine countries that were surveyed. The average Canadian uses more than 1,400 cubic metres of water per year, compared to only 300 for Sweden, 230 for the U.K., and 130 for Denmark. In other words, on a per capita basis, Canadians use more than ten times as much water as the average Dane. But the countries that do use water more efficiently do so because they pay a higher price for it. In Denmark, water is priced at $2.25 a cubic metre. In Japan it's more than $5.00 per cubic metre. In Canada, the average price for residential water consumption is around $0.40, a clear example of the Tragedy of the Commons at work — people tend to overuse resources when they do not have to bear the full cost of using them.

In addition to putting a price on water to discourage waste, there is a growing consensus that significant resources need to be spent in developing a water infrastructure worldwide. The global water market, with an estimated annual revenue of around $500 billion, is expected to grow to nearly $1 trillion by 2020. And it's this investment wave that is creating truly remarkable opportunities for our entrepreneurs.

ONE OF THE GREATEST HEALTH challenges the world faces today is to provide clean drinking water to communities across the globe. The World Health Organization (WHO) estimates that as many as a billion people still live without access to clean drinking water, and diarrhea, a common symptom of disease contracted through contaminated water, still kills as many as 1.5 million children a year. So cost-effective water purification technologies are in high demand, particularly for communities in developing countries.

Canada has the potential to be a leader in the development of water purification technologies. In fact, one of the world's most prominent water treatment companies, Zenon Environmental, was based in Ontario. Founded by Guelph engineering professor Andrew Benedek in 1980, Zenon revolutionized water processing and purification technologies by manufacturing ultrafiltration membranes that trapped particulates such as bacteria and chemicals. The technology, which became known as "reverse osmosis" technology, offered a potential alternative to chemical treatment of drinking water.

By 1995 the company had developed a viable product, but there was one big problem: it was four times more expensive than traditional water purification technologies. Over four years Benedek and his team managed to squeeze costs — by increasing output, reducing energy costs, and scaling manufacturing — until the product was price-competitive with conventional technologies. A series of well-publicized water system failures — most notably in Walkerton, Ontario, where at least seven people died from drinking contaminated water — put clean water on the public agenda. Zenon was well positioned to capitalize on this renewed interest in the public water system, and used the opportunity to build a truly global company, selling its solutions to markets around the world. In 2006, ten years after developing its flagship technology, the company was bought by General Electric for $760 million.

Around the same time that Benedek started Zenon, another Canadian entrepreneur named Hank Vander Laan bought a small company called Trojan Metal Works. Based in London, Ontario, Trojan owned an interesting piece of intellectual property — UV treatment that inactivated microorganisms in drinking water. Recognizing an extraordinary business opportunity, Vander Laan then turned to developing UV systems for large municipal waste-water facilities, and later for municipal drinking water. In the 1990s, he took the company public on the Toronto Stock Exchange. Trojan continued to grow into the early part of this decade, until, like Zenon, it was eventually acquired. Trojan still runs a global company from its operational base in London, Ontario, with annual sales in the hundreds of millions of dollars.

The presence of two highly successful water companies in southern Ontario has created a kind of "water cluster," spinning out a network of skilled employees and executives as well as attracting investors to the field. A number of people at Zenon went on to found other companies in the clean-tech and water sectors, adding much-needed depth of management experience, as well as new capital, to Canada's growing water industry. John Coburn, who was the number two at Zenon, helped fund Toronto–based EnviroTower — a company that provides a water purification system for office cooling towers — and was for a time its CEO. He also launched a water-based venture capital fund called XPV Capital. And Guelph–based Biorem Technologies has seen a number of former senior Zenon employees in senior management positions and on the board of directors.

This strength in purification has positioned Canada well to prosper in new areas of the water market, some of which may turn out to be even bigger opportunities.

WHILE WATER PURIFICATION DEFINED the first wave of innovation in the industry, water conservation, which is perhaps an even larger commercial opportunity, is likely to define the next wave. Water purification is still a more major issue in the developing world, where often the water infrastructure has not been built or is spotty, and clean water can be hard to come by. In developed countries such as Canada, the challenge is more about ensuring that the existing infrastructure is properly maintained. And so conserving water has become a big business opportunity, and has given rise to a new generation of Canadian water enterprises. Much of the focus is on upgrading and fixing our aging water infra-structure. This opportunity is attracting companies like Echologics, a Toronto–based leader in detecting leaks in municipal water pipes.

An estimated 34 percent of all water is lost through leaks in local water mains. Occasionally a leak can turn into an open chasm, bringing a city block to a standstill and needlessly wasting a tremendous amount of water and energy. Appreciating the value of the water that is lost to leaks, Mark Bracken, CEO of Echologics, designed a system that would allow for quick, accurate, and effec-tive leak detection.

Bracken is not an obvious candidate for a water CEO. After all, his background is in acoustics. But this knowledge gave him a special advantage in understand-ing how to detect ruptures in water pipes. When water leaks it makes a hissing sound. Sometimes the sound is faint or muffled by other sounds, but a leak is always audible. Bracken realized that detecting this sound could provide a means to identify weaknesses in the infra-structure more easily, accurately, and cost-effectively. He set out to develop a system that sends acoustic waves between two fire hydrants. Because sound waves move at a constant speed, Bracken's technology can determine where a leak is happening with a high degree of preci-sion. In the past, finding a leak entailed digging up an entire city block, obviously at great expense and an even greater disturbance to the local community. Now a leak can be identified down to a few feet before the digging starts.

Working with the National Research Council of Canada, Echologics has now developed a system to determine the thickness of water pipes, which allows the company to pinpoint weaknesses in the infrastructure and estimate where leaks might happen in the future. Given that much of Canada's water infrastructure was built before the Second World War, this kind of intelligence could save municipalities millions of dollars.

Echologics is only one Canadian company that has made major strides forward in leak detection analysis. Together with companies like Calgary–based Pure Technologies, they are creating a new Canadian hub of expertise in this growing area. Perhaps they will form the kind of cluster that saw Zenon and Trojan enjoy such success and spin off so much talent.

This new industry is in part a testament to Canada's leadership in the growing water industry. Not only have we been blessed with unparalleled amounts of fresh water, we are invested in providing safe drinking water to communities across the country (albeit with a few notable, and unfortunate, exceptions). But for many countries, providing safe drinking water is a huge challenge due to the lack of access to fresh water. And so more and more communities and countries are turning to our oceans, which hold 97 percent of the earth's water but cannot safely be consumed — yet.

"IT'S A GOOD THING THEY'RE not in retail," my friend commented, as we searched for Saltworks, a Vancouver–based desalination company. The job of finding Saltworks' headquarters was complicated by the fact that the office is situated in the docklands, which were in lockdown in anticipation of the 2010 Winter Olympics. Just to get to the street required passing a security check and showing photo ID. And once we'd made it through, finding the company proved to be no easy task. After asking around, we were finally directed to an industrial building tucked away down a small alley near the water. A small homespun sign that read "Saltworks Receiving" greeted us at the door.

Despite the difficulty in finding them, for the last few months the world has been beating a path to Saltworks' door. Ever since *The Economist* wrote a profile of their novel desalination technology, Saltworks has been the subject of attention from potential customers, investors, and the media. All of this interest is due to the fact that this little company tucked away in the docklands of Vancouver may just have a viable answer to the world's water woes.

For many parts of the world where fresh water is scarce, desalination is viewed as an essential solution to shortages in clean drinking water. Currently desalination is used in more than one hundred countries worldwide, and is expected to account for global expenditures of roughly $80 billion between 2005 and 2015. Many water-starved nations are already relying heavily on desalination, including countries in the Middle East, as well as Australia. And China and India will likely turn to desalination to provide water for their growing populations.

Today there are really only two commercial technologies for water desalination, and both have serious drawbacks. The first technology requires extremely high pressure to force seawater through membrane filters; the second technique uses evaporation and condensation. What they have in common is extremely high energy needs. This energy intensity adds significant electricity costs, and results in increased greenhouse gas emissions. It's ironic that the demand for these plants — driven in part by climate change, which is causing water deprivation — may in turn become a new source of greenhouse gas emissions. So for a number of reasons a race is on to find a more energy-efficient way to desalinate water.

Saltworks' founders Ben Sparrow and Joshua Zoshi met at Simon Fraser University. Sparrow had been a senior project manager at BC Hydro, where he oversaw power plant rehabilitation. But he had a secret passion for thermodynamics, which led him to come up with the idea of using thermo-ionic energy to create what he calls a "seawater battery." Sparrow decided to take a Master's in Business Administration at Simon Fraser University in part to hone his business skills to launch this new venture. There, he met Joshua Zoshi and the two began working together. A few years after graduating, the pair entered their business plan into the New Ventures BC competition in 2008, and won first prize overall as well as a sustainability prize. They received $160,000 in prize money, which provided the first capital investment for their new company.

The day I arrive, Sparrow is busy at his computer, fully immersed in his work. When he jumps up to meet me, I notice he looks the part of the young scientist, his boyish features accentuated by slightly dishevelled brown hair. The office looks to be part laboratory and part demo plant, which is basically what it is. The boardroom where I am given the company presentation is spare and undecorated; there is only a small wooden table and a couple of chairs. The rest of the office is equally simple and unadorned. It reminds me that despite all of the international attention the company has received, it's less than two years old. But for a company like Saltworks, none of that really matters. What does matter is the complicated science experiment of pipes and plastic containers that takes up much of the floor space. This is their first pilot plant, which is expected to produce 1,000 litres of desalinated water a day. It's an important step to developing their first commercial plant, which they plan to open later this year.

Sparrow leads me through the process with pride. The pilot plant represents years of theoretical work coming to fruition, and he is clearly excited. Using what they call a "thermo-ionic energy conversion system," Saltworks claims to be able to reduce the use of electrical energy by 80 percent compared to other commercial desalination technologies. The process evaporates seawater by spraying the water onto a black surface that naturally captures solar energy. This creates a highly concentrated stream of salt water with roughly 18 percent salinity, as opposed to regular seawater, which has a salinity of 3.5 percent. The highly concentrated stream of water is then pumped into a chamber along with three units of regular seawater, then separated from two vessels of regular seawater by a material made fundamentally from treated polystyrene, which acts as an "ion bridge." The ion bridge allows positively charged ions to pass through one vessel and negatively charged ions to pass through the other. Because salt is made up of two ions — sodium, which is positively charged, and chlorine, which is negatively charged — the highly concentrated water thus equilibrates its two neighbouring vessels of water, sending positive ions to one and negative ions to another. The resulting two chambers are then exposed again to regular salt water with an ion bridge, which draws out sodium and chlorine, thus reducing the salinity of the resulting stream of seawater.

The beauty of the process is that it requires very little external energy and no chemicals, resulting in lower operating costs. The main energy source comes from dry air — evaporating salt water to produce the concentrated saltwater fuel. And because the system is low pressure, they can replace expensive stainless steel, which is used in most desalination plants, for cheaper plastic parts, thus reducing capital costs and making these plants more affordable to build.

The next step for the company is to scale the plant to 5,000 litres a day, and then build a larger plant that can produce 20,000 litres or more of desalinated water. If they succeed, the name Saltworks will be a lot better known in the future, and Ben Sparrow and Joshua Zoshi will have found a solution to one of the greatest challenges humanity faces today.

WHILE WATER HAS A DIRECT impact on human life by providing drinking water for human consumption, water for agriculture and manufacturing, and energy through electricity, it also plays a critical role in providing the aquatic ecosystems for countless species. Much of Canada's natural capital is tied up in these watery ecosystems. Just as the tangible economic value of lumber can sometimes blind us to the forest's vast natural capital in the form of biodiversity, the value of water as a resource can sometimes shroud the importance it has to other living things.

A few years ago I had the opportunity to go on a fishing trip to Haida Gwaii (formerly known as the Queen Charlotte Islands), a land of ancient rainforests and teeming oceans. Haida Gwaii is central to the famous migratory route for B.C. salmon. After their time at sea, the salmon return to the rivers where they were born to spawn a new generation of fish. Given Haida Gwaii's strategic location, a huge number of those fish pass by the islands on their way to the rivers of British Columbia and Alaska. Over time, though, their populations have decreased.

Again, the story is not simple. There are any number of causes for declines in fish population, not the least of which is overfishing (and I was pleased to see that the number of Chinook salmon that sports fishermen could take was limited and strictly monitored). Aquacul-ture is also a factor, as wild populations are at risk of catching diseases from locally farmed salmon; indeed, many of the pink salmon we caught were covered in sea lice, likely a result of coming into contact with Atlantic salmon raised in open pens all across the Pacific coast.

But climate change is also emerging as a major influence in the decline of wild salmon populations. At the time of spawning, when salmon must make a final journey upriver, higher river temperatures appear to deplete the fish's energy, as well as increase bacterial and fungal infections, which have an impact on the fish's immune systems. Sockeye salmon, for example, are affected by temperatures of over 18°C, and will fre-quently die of thermal shock in water warmer than 23°C. In major migratory rivers, such as the Fraser, the water temperature is sometimes already in excess of 20°C.

Whatever the reasons, there is no question that the B.C. salmon fisheries are in decline, as evidenced by the near collapse of the once plentiful Fraser River sockeye salmon run in July 2009; only 1.7 million of an expected 10.6 to 13 million spawned that year. This is not only an ecological crisis, it's an economic one as well. The value of the Pacific salmon to the B.C. economy peaked in the late 1980s and has since decreased. And salmon is not only critical to the commercial fisheries, but also is a centrepiece of the province's $1.4 billion ecotourism industry.

It's possible that British Columbia's salmon may be going the way of the Atlantic cod. This pattern has been repeated in oceans around the world. In her book *Sea Sick*, Canadian author and journalist Alanna Mitchell calls the alarming disappearance of fisheries "a marine Armageddon." She cites a 2006 *Science* article, which predicts a "total collapse of all commercial fisheries by 2048 unless practices change." Never before has the importance of understanding the pressures on fish species been greater.

A critical first step to finding better ways to manage our fisheries is to understand what, in fact, is happening to our fish. Providing information on the survival of fish species is exactly the role of companies like Lotek Wireless Inc. Founded by engineer Jim Lotimer, Newmarket–based Lotek is one of the world's leading biotelemetry companies.

In the 1980s, Lotimer worked for the Ontario Ministry of the Environment, where he developed tools used to track animals and occasionally did the tracking himself. When the Ontario government pulled its funding in 1984, Lotimer founded Lotek. During the first few years, Lotimer trekked out into the wilderness to do field research; an old company photo shows a bearded

Jim Lotimer, looking more Grizzly Adams than company executive, in the snowy woods with a tagged and tranquilized black bear at his feet. But for the next twenty-five years he honed considerable business acumen, and the company become a hi-tech leader, developing new technology that helped define the industry. Along the way, Lotek recorded numerous firsts. For example, the company created CART, the first integrated, dynamically switched, coded, acoustic radio fish tag. The company has also won countless awards, including the 2003 Canada Export Award from the Department of Foreign Affairs and International Trade. Today Lotek employs more than a hundred employees with offices in Newmarket, Ontario; St. John's, Newfoundland; and Dorset, England.

Lotimer's easygoing manner masks a strong ambition and will. Despite his serene exterior, an intense inner drive gives him a quiet authority and the leadership presence required to navigate a complicated market environment. In part, Jim's leadership speaks to a sense of balance and perspective that he brings to his life. He blends an environmental ethic — he makes time for annual canoe trips into the wilderness — with a passion for business, and his understanding of technology has served him well as the company's products have become more complex and hi-tech.

Lotek has built a profitable niche by developing sophisticated tools for what the company calls "biotelemetry."

"We develop advanced equipment and analytical techniques that, when placed on free-ranging wild animals and fish, provide the world with the knowledge required to scientifically validate and assess the environment — from the perspective of the animal," Lotimer explains.

Using sophisticated radio, acoustic, and satellite technologies, Lotek Wireless was able to provide researchers with the tools to better understand how fish, birds, and mammals live, as well as the factors that threaten them.

Lotek's equipment has been central to understanding how our oceans work. For example, their technology enabled Stanford University marine sciences professor Barbara Block to discover that what was previously thought to be two distinct geographical groups of tuna (one living primarily in the West Atlantic, one in the East) were in fact one, with individuals migrating across the ocean. This kind of information unlocks new ways of understanding the species and offers valuable information that will be critical to learning how we might better co-exist with the species in the future.

In the past these tools have been used primarily to ensure that human industry does not encroach upon wild fish or animal populations, especially in places like the Fraser River, which is both heavily used by people and critical to British Columbia's salmon run. But new markets for conservation science and animal telemetry are set to grow in coming years, fuelled by climate change research.

One example of this kind of research is the Ocean Tracking Network (OTN), based out of Dalhousie University in Halifax. This $168 million project was funded in part by a grant from the Canada Foundation for Innovation (CFI), which promises to "unite the finest marine scientists in the world in the most comprehensive and revolutionary examination of marine life and ocean conditions ever undertaken." Lotek and two other biotelemetry companies — Nova Scotia–based Amirix and Satlantic Inc. — are industrial partners in OTN, providing the technology that will fuel the research. If OTN is successful, it may well open the door for further studies around the world to understand what is happening to our fish populations in this time of unprecedented climate change.

Jim Lotimer's vision is to help the world measure and preserve its natural capital. He believes that capturing information about the natural world is a vital part of a healthy interaction with other species. This data helps us determine the viability of those populations, and the stresses that are being put on them by humans and our actions.

JUST AS WAS TRUE IN THE CASE OF FORESTS, it is perhaps time for us to reconsider the value of water and all of its uses. As long as we continue to see water as a cheap commodity, we will naturally overuse it. But if we place a proper value on the resource, not only will we use it less wastefully, we will drive further technical innovations that will ensure we have access to it in the future. And so getting the price right is a step toward innovation, conservation, and sustainability in water, as it is for most of our vital resources. Nowhere is it more relevant than in the way we use and manage electricity.

Chapter Three

ELECTRIC AVENUE

On August 14, 2003, at 4:15 p.m. EDT, the lights went out. I was at work, busy typing on my computer, when the systems went down. At first I thought it was just my computer that had crashed, but rebooting it didn't help. And then I heard other people in the office complaining that their computers and lights had shut down too. This must be a building-wide problem, we decided. Eventually rumours began to trickle in that we were part of a larger event.

I remember driving back home along Toronto's Don Valley Parkway, which is normally busy but on that day was clogged with cars. With so many people leaving work at the same time, traffic was at a standstill. For most of us that was okay, as the radio was one of the last remaining communication tools available. What we learned was that a massive energy failure had spread across multiple states and provinces, affecting 55 million energy users across northeastern North America. Authorities were scrambling to find the cause of the problem and to assure a jittery public that all was being done to fix it. But as time ticked on, the story became more confusing. Authorities could not even agree on where the problem had originated. Everyone thought someone else was to blame. Then Prime Minister Jean Chrétien insisted that the cause was a lightning strike in New York; there were rumours that the source of the blackout was a nuclear plant in Pennsylvania; the governor of New York pointed his finger at Canada.

Along the roads of downtown Toronto, a kind of controlled anarchy took hold. The traffic lights had all gone out, and Good Samaritans jumped into the fray, acting as traffic cops to keep the cars moving in an orderly way. The streets were jammed with thousands of subway riders walking home, their work bags slung over their shoulders. It was all a little chaotic; but then again, it all held together surprisingly well.

When I got home I tried to call my family, but the cell phone services were out of commission. Fortunately

I knew that they were safely tucked away on Four Winds island in Georgian Bay, which isn't connected to the power grid. They were likely some of the few people in Ontario oblivious to the great commotion happening to the south.

That night I walked the streets of downtown Toronto, which were eerily dark and quiet. People had pulled out their flashlights to make their way through the streets. Bars were doing a booming business as locals congregated to discuss the unusual event, parking their cars to point toward the bars so that the headlights could illuminate the interiors. The city had transformed into a communal village; people passing each other on the street, their faces shrouded in the night, would say a reassuring hello. For the first time in decades, the stars were clearly visible in the night sky over the city.

That night, Ontario premier Ernie Eves declared a state of emergency. Consumers who had regained power were asked to refrain from using air condition- ing or turning on their televisions until the power had been fully restored. The Niagara Falls generating sta- tion began to work at full tilt to compensate for the lost power, while authorities struggled to get the system up and running again. Still, it was another five days before life essentially returned to normal.

What we experienced that day was the collapse of a vast, integrated electricity grid. It happened, we now know, as a result of the shutdown of a power facility in Ohio, which put extra strain on high-voltage transmission lines. When lines heated up, they began to sag, then came into contact with the tree branches that hung underneath the electricity distribution corridor. That contact caused power to be rerouted onto other high-voltage lines, which suffered a similar fate. As the electricity corridors began to fail, power plants had to be shut down. Eventually the problem cascaded, affecting the entire eastern electrical grid. At the height of the blackout, 265 power plants had shut down and much of eastern North America was in the dark.

This incident was of course a great education to most North American energy consumers, who previously had little or no interest in power and electricity. What they saw was an alarming picture of a phenomenally complicated, interconnected system being brought to its knees. This aging and archaic system — what's been called the largest machine in the world — had proven vulnerable to catastrophic failure.

The great blackout of 2003 helped underline some of the vulnerabilities of the current electricity grid. But that grid is an extension of an aging infrastructure that was built many years ago based on a series of assumptions about electricity use. In general, it is a system that favours large power facilities, mostly situated in relatively remote locations, that can produce and distribute vast amounts of power through high-voltage corridors. The system is essentially unidirectional in that power is created for the consumer, who typically pays a flat rate that does not fluctuate based on market forces. In effect, the consumer has little connection to the process. It's amazing, in a way, that this kind of system was designed by modern capitalist societies, because in some sense it has all of the intelligent design of a 1970s Soviet-style power grid.

The blackout created a new awareness of this vast and complicated system, which includes more than a thousand power plants across North America with an estimated value of more than $800 billion. But an awareness of other problems caused by our current means of power generation has also been steadily growing. Most people now understand that our power industry is a major contributor to local air pollution, responsible for 20 percent of all sulphur dioxide emissions, 11 percent of all nitrogen oxides, and 25 percent of all mercury emissions. An estimated 21,000 Canadians die prematurely every year on account of air pollution; clearly our power generation industry is a major contributor to this mortality rate. And with a growing public interest in climate change, the power industry has also come under increasing scrutiny for contributing 22 percent of all CO_2 emissions, second only to the transportation industry.

In addition, the considerable expenses associated with system management and upgrades will require our governments to look again at the most efficient way to provide electricity for consumers. In the last few years the cost of building a new nuclear reactor has grown from $2,500 per kilowatt to as high as $7,000 per kilowatt, a staggering sum. And while energy options such as coal are much cheaper, they are also the largest contributors to local air pollution and climate change. Despite the chatter about the imminent possibility of producing "clean coal," in reality it is much too costly to be considered a viable option today. So, in practice, there really are very few easy choices in power generation; almost everything comes with a downside.

In addition, the cost of maintaining aging transmission lines is soaring. Much of our electricity infrastructure is now more than fifty years old, and as time marches on it will become increasingly vulnerable to failure. We can expect to see more events such as the transformer explosion of July 2008, which forced the evacuation of nine hundred people from a Toronto neighbourhood. But confronting these issues also creates an opportunity to reimagine a new electricity system of the future — one that will be greener, more efficient, and more robust. It's a complicated puzzle with many parts. But in some respects it is leading us back in time to a distributed electricity network that comes closer to the way we created power in earlier times.

SURREY IS ONE OF THE LARGEST cities in Canada — large in terms of population and in terms of sheer geographical size. That's what I learned when I went to visit Endurance Wind Power. When I got in the cab just outside of Vancouver, I asked the driver to take me to Surrey. "Surrey is a very large place," the cabbie answered in a soft Indian accent. So I was to discover as we drove for close to an hour, first through suburbs and urban sprawl, then eventually through farmland, finally landing at a nondescript office building at the far reaches of the city. I was there to meet Glenn Johnson, CEO of Endurance, a leading manufacturer of small wind turbines.

When Johnson greeted me he apologized for the state of the office, which was at the tail-end of a construction phase to expand the office space and manufacturing facilities. I was immediately impressed by Johnson's energy, sense of direction, and confidence. Trim and well dressed, he was crackling with energy; it was as if he was permanently hooked up to one of his own systems.

Like many of the entrepreneurs in this book, Johnson had spearheaded other successful ventures before
founding Endurance. In the 1990s he built a small communications distribution company called Comsource
Broadband Technologies into a corporation with revenues
of $75 million. Later he founded a merchant bank called
Glace Capital Corporation. In the course of researching
new investments for Glace, he came upon a wind technology developed by two engineers that had been exten-
sively tested with excellent results but never aggressively
marketed. Johnson was able to acquire the technology,
raise capital, construct a small manufacturing facility, and
put together a marketing plan to sell the turbines interna-
tionally. He was also able to convince the two engineers to
join him and continue to be a part of a growing team.[4]

Although the market for wind power has been
increasing dramatically for the past twenty years — aver-
aging annual growth rates of approximately 20 percent
— the industry has focused almost exclusively on large
wind turbines capable of generating one megawatt of

---

4   Like many of the entrepreneurs in this book, Glenn Johnson was
uncomfortable being the focus of this story. In a note to me, he said:
"Although I am the leader of the team, largest shareholder, and front
man, I acquired the technology with other partners and we retained the
designing engineers as partners in Endurance and they are still with us
today. Basically there is no 'I' in team, and both my partner team and my
employee team are fabulous!" It's worth noting here, because the hallmark
of many great entrepreneurs is that they are excellent team builders, and
behind many of these people are other remarkable individuals.

power or more. So the race for innovation and efficiency has thus far been measured by size. Turbine size is one indication. The current record holder is German company Enercon, whose E-126 is rated at 6 megawatts, has a 125-metre rotor blade, and is capable of powering around two thousand homes. The scale of developments has also grown; typically many large turbines are erected on wind farms that replicate conventional power facilities in size. For example, the staggering 197 MW wind farm built by Calgary–based Canadian Hydro Developers covers virtually all of Wolfe Island, which is at the eastern edge of Lake Ontario and can be seen clearly from Kingston.

These types of large-scale wind developments have begun to attract conventional power producers. In August 2009 Canadian Hydro elicited a hostile $654 million takeover bid from TransAlta, Alberta's largest electricity producer. This proposed takeover comes on the heels of a number of acquisitions of independent Canadian wind companies in 2008 and 2009 — companies such as Ventus, which was purchased by the European giant GDF Suez in 2008. It's a clear sign that the wind industry is evolving; what once was an entrepreneurial cottage industry has become the domain of the largest energy companies on the planet.

But even as Canada succeeds in building wind power development companies, the turbines are generally built elsewhere, mostly offshore in Germany or Denmark. These countries virtually created the modern wind industry in the 1980s, and therefore developed the special skills and know-how that allowed them to become the leading suppliers of wind technology worldwide. Canada, late to the wind game, never really developed any manufacturing expertise in large wind turbines. And that is why a possible renewal of smaller scale wind energy holds a special interest, as it may allow us to get into the market not only as developers but also as manufacturers of the equipment. Certainly that is what Endurance is hoping.

The market for small wind energy has been fragmented to date, without enough critical mass to build a real manufacturing operation. Governments have typically avoided providing long-term power purchase agreements to small turbine operators, as the amount of power generated is not significant enough to justify the contract. So small wind was seen only as a niche market that made sense for energy users such as farmers or for those who lived in remote locations and were not connected to the energy grid.

The market for small wind power became a little more interesting with the introduction of the concept of net metering, which allows small energy producers to sell electricity back to the grid. This development marked a major turning point in the evolution of our electricity system. All of a sudden power was no longer unidirectional, and individual consumers could become producers as well, selling any excess electricity at a preset price. Still, those prices tended to be modest and unappealing. But in the last few years the landscape has changed again with the introduction of "feed-in tariffs," such as the one in Ontario's Green Energy Act, which provide an enhanced price to renewable energy producers. Consumers who installed a small wind turbine on their property could finally get an attractive guaranteed price for their electricity. Some feed-in tariffs, such as the one announced in the United Kingdom, put an even higher price on electricity generated from smaller wind turbines. On account of these kinds of programs (or, alternatively, various tax credits offered by many states in the U.S.), the economics looked much better, and small wind, formerly the poor cousin of large wind energy, began to take off.

Enter Glenn Johnson. Johnson had either the foresight or the good luck to tie his company's success to feed-in tariffs. His machines, unlike those of many of his competitors, are engineered to plug directly into the grid. As the market swings toward grid-connected energy, he's found himself in the right place at the right time.

Walking with Johnson around the Endurance office, you get the impression of an entrepreneur who knows he has a tiger by the tail. He's just expanded the office, and acquired a new wind technology company to allow him to get into the space in the market for power generation that's above 10 kilowatts and below 100 kilowatts, where turbines in the tens of thousands of dollars can produce enough electricity to power multiple homes, commercial properties, or farms. The day I visited the Endurance office also happened to be the first day on the job for the new head of international sales.

Johnson knows he needs to grow the company quickly, but predicting where the growth will come from is hard. With the advent of government support and consumer interest, small wind has now become a huge worldwide market, and Endurance is one of a handful of companies that is truly ready to compete. But the scale of the opportunity also comes with its own challenges, and Johnson understands that his success will depend in part on keeping his team focused. With an international opportunity of potentially staggering size, it will be important to choose carefully where to spend their time and capital for the best results.

For now, Endurance seems to have a clear market advantage. Their turbines are the most efficient in low to medium wind, which accounts for the majority of all wind locations. Although the machines are designated by their maximum wind speed potential, the amount of energy they harvest in reality is a small fraction of the total, as the wind is rarely blowing at the ideal velocity.

Johnson is confident that his machines can compete with any around the world because of the amount of energy they provide for the cost, the ultimate determiner of the financial payback and return on investment for the user. And Endurance machines are reliable and hardy. Features such as a dual disk brake, which can stop the turbine when wind speeds become too fast, increases both the safety and longevity of the system. They are also made to be quiet, which is critical in an industry that sometimes attracts backlash from local communities. Johnson ensures that Endurance abides by the highest manufacturing standards, even going as far as making their own shipping crates. He wants to know that he is in control of all the variables of his business, and this attention to detail may be the thing that sets the company apart going forward.

All of these product attributes, along with a seasoned team, positions Endurance at the head of the pack in a new area of renewable energy that the huge industrial players — including multinational behemoths such as General Electric and Siemens — have largely ignored. But if the sector takes off, as it looks like it may, those larger companies will surely come knocking. For small wind — less constrained by "NIMBY" opposition that has caused trouble for many large wind projects, and more accessible to the grid than large turbines, which often require significant transmission infrastructure — is in a way the ideal form of renewable, distributed energy. So for now, Glenn Johnson's prospects look pretty good.

Johnson offers me a ride back to the airport, but my cab driver has agreed to wait for me, amazed at his good fortune to drive someone all the way across Surrey and back. As we travel back to the airport, I look around the Surrey countryside and see the potential for companies like Endurance come to life. While large wind turbine installations are attracting greater resistance from locals and residents, the small wind market is virtually untapped and almost infinite in its potential. I can imagine small wind turbines all across these farms, offices, and subdivisions, their blades spinning out the kilowatts, providing electricity right where it is needed and used. It's an exciting vision — a distributed electricity grid that is powered locally by the people who use it, and that fits the needs of growing communities such as Surrey, B.C.

IF SMALL WIND SHOWS REMARKABLE potential for a distributed renewable energy future, the technology that is even more ideal to fulfill this vision is solar. Because solar panels have relatively small footprints, are visually inoffensive, and can be installed on rooftops, a lot of people are banking on the sun as the ultimate renewable energy source for the twenty-first century. If this happens, it will reinforce the long-held bond between humanity and our ultimate energy source.

As long as humanity has existed, we have been by necessity a civilization of sun worshippers. That illuminating orb, 150 million kilometres away from us, has brought order to our days and years, and provided the essential spark for all existence on this planet. From the Egyptian god Re, Helios of the Greeks, and the Roman god Apollo, the sun has always held a place of veneration and acted as a central guiding force for most of human history.

In 1200 astronomer and mathematician Nicolaus Copernicus posited that the sun was the true centre of the solar system, not the earth. And later, in the seventeenth century, astronomer and physicist Galileo Galilei was found guilty by the Inquisition and condemned to house arrest for daring to support Copernicus's theory publicly (Copernicus presented his theory as a piece of fiction to give himself some deniability). But in later years the sun has not been given its due. Today humanity lives as if it could make do without that distant light bulb in the sky. With coal and nuclear power, we sometimes take the sun for granted, even though it is indirectly the source of almost all of our energy. Through its ability to cause evaporation, it provides hydroelectric power; through the process of photosynthesis, it provides all of our fossil fuels; through heat distribution, it creates wind energy; and by heating the earth, it can provide thermal energy for our homes.

Despite the importance of the sun as *the* energy source for planet Earth, we generate a strikingly small amount of energy directly from it; in fact today less than 0.05 percent of all the world's electricity is solar-generated. But the potential is huge. Every hour the Earth receives enough solar radiation to power all of humanity's electricity needs for a year. The problem of course is not volume, it's price.

Though photovoltaic energy — the technology that converts the sun's energy into electricity — has been available for some time, it has never been at a cost that would allow it to compete with indirect solar energy such as coal (which sounds counter-intuitive: if you think solar energy is too expensive, grow plants with it, let them sit for millions of years under perfectly pressurized conditions, come back and dig them up, and burn them in a furnace to turn a turbine and create electricity — then it will be a lot cheaper!).

This is not for lack of trying. Significant efforts have been made over the years to make solar-generated electricity a more commercially attractive energy source. The term photovoltaic itself derives from two sources: the Greek word for light (*phōs*), and Italian inventor Alessandro Volta, who discovered the electric cell and after whom the basic unit of energy, the volt, was named. The photovoltaic effect was first discovered in 1839 by French physicist Alexandre-Edmond Becquerel. Becquerel used a device he had created called a phosphoroscope, which allowed him to see the effect of light on certain materials.

It was not until 1883 that American inventor Charles Fritts built the first working solar cell by wrapping a thin layer of gold around a conductive material called selenium. But Fritz's device had efficiencies of only 1 percent, and it was not until 1954 that experiments at Bell Laboratories in the United States led to the development of a solar cell with efficiencies of 6 percent.

Since then, efforts have been made to increase the efficiencies of solar cells while decreasing the cost of production to make them cost-competitive with conventional energy. The major breakthrough, or more likely series of breakthroughs, that would allow solar energy to compete with grid power has yet to occur. But prices are coming

down, and the prospect of solar power achieving cost
parity with grid electricity gets closer every day.

One person who is trying to expedite that process
is Dr. John MacDonald, CEO of Vancouver–based Day 4
Energy — a company named for the fourth day of creation, on which God created light. Dr. MacDonald brings
an impressive combination of academic, scientific, and
business credentials to his efforts to increase the efficiency and power output of solar power. He was an engineering professor at MIT and UBC before he founded
MacDonald Dettwiler and Associates, a space technology
company, in 1968. Over the next thirty years, the firm
was to become Canada's leading aerospace company,
with John MacDonald at the helm. In 1998 he retired
from the space industry, but within three years he was
back at it, this time as co-founder of Day 4 Energy.

In his new role, MacDonald doubles as CEO and
solar power evangelist. "The energy business and the
technology behind it will be the major thing that happens in human civilization in the twenty-first century,"
he proclaims. "We will change our energy system. We
will be forced to change it." MacDonald believes that by
mid-century our energy will be dominated by renewable
power. But he knows that for it to get there, the cost of
renewable power must come down, and he thinks Day 4
can help get it there.

Day 4's technology promises 25 percent higher power density, along with improved performance when cells are exposed to shade or snow. The critical piece of the company's technology is referred to as the Day 4 Electrode, which results in a 6 percent increase in power output and eliminates steps in the manufacturing process, thus increasing plant efficiencies and reducing costs. In a game of inches, where solar is competing worldwide with every other imaginable energy option, these small gains can have an enormous impact on the viability of photovoltaics.

While solar-generated electricity is coming down in price, other ways of harnessing the sun's energy are already cost competitive. One example is solar thermal technology. Unlike solar photovoltaic technology, solar thermal uses heat properties to create energy without having to convert it into electricity. The most common use of this is for hot water heating, which accounts on average for 20 percent of the energy of a typical household. Businesses that use a lot of hot water — such as restaurants, hotels, or laundromats — are also excellent candidates for solar thermal hot water heating.

Solar thermal energy has been in use around the world for years, especially in warm climates. In colder climates, however, where temperatures dip below freezing, more complicated systems — using glycol as a heat conductor instead of water — are required. But the challenge with this method has been to prevent the glycol from boiling when temperatures get too hot.

Steve Harrison, director of Queen's University's Solar Calorimetry Lab in Kingston, Ontario, is one of the world's leading experts on solar thermal technology. His patented improvements to solar thermal hot water heating technology, including a valve to release excess heat to prevent glycol from overheating, have been integrated into EnerWorks, a solar manufacturer based in Dorchester, Ontario. EnerWorks products are CSA–certified, easy to install, and with a powerful array of government tax credits offer reasonable paybacks even at Canada's latitude.

Solar thermal technology is also able to provide cooling. Working again with Steve Harrison, EnerWorks has developed solar thermal air conditioning systems, opening up a potentially vast new market. Solar radiation is not always aligned with heating requirements in northern countries, because heat is most useful in the winter when solar radiation is scarce. Solar and air conditioning, however, are very well aligned, since solar radiation is of course strongest when the need for air conditioning is greatest. Using a heat exchanger, solar energy can provide cooling for commercial buildings, opening a market of enormous size and commercial potential.

Another approach to making solar power more affordable is being advanced by Ottawa–based Menova. They are developing a system of parabolic mirrors that can track the sun's movement and direct concentrated energy on small high-efficiency solar cells — the kind that are used in space and have efficiencies in the 40-percent range, as opposed to the 17 percent range of regular solar cells. The excess heat can be used for thermal applications, making the electrical cells more efficient. These systems then produce both electricity and heat, and are perfect for applications where both are required. Walmart stores are just one example of an early customer.

Although most of the pieces of this system are already available in one form or another, it may still be some time before we can once again become a heliotropic society. If it does happen, it would fulfill the eighty-year-old prediction made by Thomas Edison, the inventor of the light bulb, when he said: "I'd put my money on the sun and solar energy. What a source of power! I hope we don't have to wait till oil and coal run out before we tackle that."

WHILE SOLAR AND WIND POWER ARE beginning to have an impact on energy production in Canada, they do not yet represent a significant percentage of our overall power generation. Another potential renewable energy source has, though — hydro power, which has long played a central role in power generation across the country. In fact, the history of hydro power in Canada stretches back to before the age of electricity. Not only did water provide the transportation needs for the canoes of the early voyageurs, but it provided the power that was essential to creating the small pulp, textile, and grain mills that were the economic centres of so many communities. I was reminded of the role that hydro played in a recent trip to Milltown, a small community equidistant between Toronto and Kingston. I was there to meet another Godsall: Terry Godsall, father of Chris, the founder of Triton Logging.

If Chris Godsall was destined to launch a green logging company, he came by it naturally. Indeed, his family is notable for its incredible interest in green businesses. Two of Chris's brothers are directly involved in launching green enterprises. His brother Jay is developing the "solar ship," a solar-powered airship that is part airplane, part helium-filled balloon, and would require a fraction of the gas required to operate a conventional aircraft. His half-brother Jonathan is now running Zumer, a site aimed at giving consumers information on the environmental performance of companies from whom they buy their products. But of all the Godsalls, Terry has perhaps the most far-reaching vision. His goal is to reactivate all of the original mills that now sit idle and unused, and recreate a vast new power source that dates back to a time before the modern era.

Terry Godsall is an environmentalist, engineer, and entrepreneur. His forty-year career has taken him from activism, to investment banking, to consulting in the forestry and energy sectors. He was involved in many significant resource projects, including the Mackenzie Valley Pipeline and the Churchill Falls and James Bay hydroelectric projects. But for the last sixteen years his interest in the environment and business has given rise to a new approach to hydroelectric power.

Terry and his partners wanted to show me a site that they considered ideal for a new way of generating power. It's a small dam, what's known as "low head" because the elevation is quite limited. In fact, as Terry explains, Ontario is littered with thousands of old mill sites, which were once the foundation of the province's economy. But when electricity came along, most of the mills fell out of use and into disrepair. Terry and his business partners want to reinvent these sites as sources of new green electricity. He calls it going "back to the future."

Conventional wisdom holds that hydro facilities under around 10 metres of head — the term used to describe the height that the water falls — are not viable for producing electricity. Indeed, very few turbine designs work well enough in these conditions to provide a compelling commercial return. So these sites have largely been left to the weeds and the trees, despite the fact that there is an estimated 5,000 megawatts of untapped low-head hydro potential in Canada.

But Terry's group has designed a new way of creating electricity from these sites. When I ask him what is at the heart of his design, he answers: "eccentricity." By placing the axel of the turbine off-centre, Terry was able to engineer a more efficient design that works in low water. It also happens to be extremely gentle on fish habitat and easy to install. With Ontario's new Green Energy Act, which includes a feed-in tariff that prices hydro at more than 13 cents a kilowatt, Terry and his team feel they have a market niche with significant commercial potential.

Ontario, like much of Canada, has been powered by water — so much so that its public energy utility was named Ontario Hydro. The history of hydroelectricity in Ontario dates back to the turn of the last century, with the creation of the Canadian Niagara Power Company. Ironically, that company, which provided vast quantities of electricity to consumers and corporations and drove the Ontario economy into the twentieth century, made obsolete the older water power mills that Terry Godsall is now trying to recommission. The small hydro dams and windmills that once provided local communities with power were eventually supplanted by mega-projects such as Churchill Falls, or enormous coal-generating plants. The big projects were able to command a critical mass that in the end also made them more economically efficient.

But those big projects are getting harder to build. The logistics are staggeringly complicated, and the projects often attract vociferous opposition from organized local interest groups, increasing construction time and expense. Beyond that, enormous mega-projects are getting harder to finance by governments labouring under the weight of public debt and managing ever-increasing costs of other public expenditures, notably health care. For these reasons, we may be moving back to a time of small. In the energy space, there are a lot of advantages to small-scale projects. They have lower capital costs, less distribution expense, less electricity loss due to distribution, less local opposition, and (usually) fewer negative environmental consequences. And they can be built and implemented more quickly.

I get a better sense of Terry's vision when he takes me to his new home at Tamworth, where he has bought an old mill on the banks of the Salmon River. Before Terry bought the property, the millhouse had fallen into complete disrepair to the point where the building was barely standing. Terry's team helped to reinforce the walls with concrete and rebuild the millhouse for Terry's living quarters. They claim it is the highest LEED building in North America. And it is a stunning display of old meets new — a visually breathtaking structure that mixes concrete, steel, and stone to create a bright and spacious living space.

But it's in the basement where Terry's vision truly comes alive. For there he has rebuilt the penstocks from the original dam and run them into a large cistern, which in turn runs through a smaller version of his new turbine design. It's a scaled-down model of what he hopes to build across Ontario.

He demonstrates how it operates. By opening a gate under the cistern, water is soon gushing through the turbine. For a moment I catch a glimpse of how Terry's eccentric vision may soon become a reality. Although it's only a demonstration model — and not yet connected to a generator to create electricity — it is an exciting step on the path to reinvigorating small hydro.

Walking out toward the river, we pass a huge carved rock, which looks like an enormous obelisk. Terry explains that this piece of art is created by Montreal artists who have a vacation property in town. Gravity will push water from the river up through the statue, like a fountain, and as it percolates through the intricately carved channels on the surface, green stones embedded in the small channels will become illuminated by the water and the sun. I look forward to seeing this work of art come to life one day, just as I look forward to seeing Terry and his partners' vision of a new beginning for a very old and vital part of Ontario's economy come to fruition.

Terry Godsall's low-head hydro project completes the picture of an electricity pendulum swinging back toward smaller scale, zero-emission energy based on water, wind, and solar power. Although the power potential in any one installation is insignificant, huge numbers of small facilities can add up to significant electricity generation. To get there, though, consumers and energy users will have to become more aware of the merits and potential of renewable energy production, and that will require a new way of selling electricity. For the battle to promote green energy is to get the consumer to understand that all electrons are not made equally.

In 2003 I took a plane up to Northern Ontario to see a working small hydro plant, a slightly larger version of Terry Godsall's low-head hydro project. It was a well-constructed 3.5 megawatt facility, generating enough electricity to power a thousand homes. It's a "run of-river" project, which means that the dam has minimal storage capacity. In this case most of the river runs over the dam, but part of it is diverted through a penstock to create power and then returned back to the river 100 metres or so later. It's an elegant solution that avoids disrupting the natural flow of the river — and the fish that live in it — while simultaneously providing clean and reliable power.

My travel companion that day was technology entrepreneur Greg Kiessling. After completing an engineering degree at the University of Waterloo, Kiessling built a company called Sitraka, which provided software solutions for large IT companies. Sitraka grew into a successful venture — the largest privately financed software company in Canada at one time — before being acquired by Quest Software in 2002. Kiessling was looking for a new sector to invest in and build companies in, and turned toward green energy.

As we were shown through the small hydro facility by one of the operators, I could tell by the nature of Greg's questions that the plant had sparked some new ideas. Tall and trim with a long distance runner's build, Kiessling has an inquisitive mind and disposition, and I could almost see the cogs in his entrepreneurial mind turning as he began to ask about how electricity was distributed. For instance, how could one sell energy directly to consumers? Or, more generally, how might one go about bundling up green energy and selling it to electricity users?

As fate would have it, Kiessling was also in touch with someone else I know pretty well — my brother, Tom Heintzman — to ask these very same questions. In fact, Tom's interest in environmental issues predates mine. In the mid-1990s he left a successful legal practice to become a counsel for the Sierra Legal Defence Fund, where he acted on behalf of individuals and small groups trying to enforce environmental rules generally against larger, well-heeled corporations with huge legal budgets. A few years later he went to work for the management consulting firm McKinsey & Company, where he represented one of Canada's largest utilities companies and a few oil sands corporations. He then went on to work in mergers and acquisitions at Zenon Environmental.

All along the way, Tom dreamed of building a sustainable company, believing that any solution to the world's environmental problems required profitable green businesses to lead the way. Tom was looking for the right opportunity when he met Greg Kiessling. It was a propitious meeting. As Tom says, "Unlike most other product categories (sports, cars, cleaning products, etc.) the environment was a completely unbranded space. Brands will be necessary to cut through the confusion of competing environmental claims, and there was opportunity to create the 'Nike of the environment.' To succeed, the brand had to be based on legitimate environmental credentials to establish trust with the consumer."

The idea of a green electricity marketing firm is relatively unusual, even counter-intuitive. Electricity is a commodity that most consumers spend little time thinking about, and understand even less. How the power is created, where it comes from, what consequences it has for the environment — these are issues that most consumers are not really tuned in to. But over the last number of years, electricity has become a topical subject, partly on account of the blackout of 2003 but also as a result of a growing awareness of how it contributes to climate change and air pollution. Bullfrog Power was well-positioned to take advantage of these trends.

Still, the challenges of selling green electricity are bedevilling. For one, since building a separate grid for renewable electricity is not practical, it's virtually impossible to separate the electrons from green projects and non-green projects into different streams. So electricity, regardless of its source, is delivered through a single electricity grid. Nevertheless, Bullfrog has succeeded in making the case for buying green power, satisfying consumers' desire to purchase green electricity, and at a systemic level using the money from its customers to pay the premium that renewable power developers have to charge to develop new low-impact generation facilities. In this sense the company has built a compelling sales proposition: spend a little more on green electricity for your home to ensure that more green electricity gets built onto the grid.

Knowing that the company would survive or fail on the strength of the message to the consumer, Bullfrog worked with the highly acclaimed Bruce Mau Design to create a powerful brand image that would attract the green consumer. So far it's worked. Bullfrog has virtually defined green marketing in Canada, and has garnered a long list of achievements and awards. As a sign of their incredible and unusual following, the company attracted 700 customers to their second anniversary bash. In addition, the company has built on this cult-like following through e-mail newsletters, lawn signs, hats, and other identifiers of the Bullfrog nation. This grassroots marketing campaign has drawn in a wide array of commercial clients, from most of the large Canadian banks, to retailer giants Walmart Canada and Mac's Convenience stores, and even companies such as Astral Media. Many businesses are keen to position themselves as green companies — especially in the minds of their increasingly discerning consumers — and buying Bullfrog Power is a good way to do that.

Bullfrog has now become a national brand, selling power to consumers in British Columbia, Alberta, Ontario, and the Maritimes. The company shows how far the environmental sector has come in such a short time, in terms of attracting talent into these new markets and competing with long-standing brands for consumers. And because they have built solid, definable product differentiation, they can steal significant market share from conventional suppliers. More importantly, Bullfrog has forced consumers to think about where their electricity comes from, and to understand the enormously complex network that is responsible for providing them this vital service. It's a critical step toward a more conscious, and conscientious, electricity consumer.

WHILE LOW CARBON ENERGY production from sources such as wind and solar and hydro is critical for our future, there is an even more compelling green energy opportunity that can yield great returns: conservation and efficiency. Throughout the twentieth century, while the world focused on dumping vast quantities of relatively cheap electrons onto ever-expanding electricity grids, we lost sight of an obvious opportunity: to use energy more efficiently. There are significant opportunities to invest in energy efficiency, and typically these investments have better economics than creating new power. Also, energy efficiency and conservation carry none of the negative consequences that almost all energy sources — even wind and solar — inevitably do.

There are a number of impediments to investing in efficiency, but probably the main one is how we price our energy. Across Canada, governments have gone out of their way to protect consumers from the full cost of power. Not only are energy users frequently shielded from some of the basic costs of electricity generation and distribution, we almost never pay for any of the external costs of energy — the immediate health and environmental costs on account of air pollution, as well as the longer term costs of climate change. Add these factors to the mix, and it is clear that our electricity and energy costs are massively subsidized. And those subsidies will limit the development of one of the most promising sources of new energy: the negawatt.

The concept of the negawatt is one of those delightful accidents of history. The word actually first appeared as a typo in a report by the Colorado Public Utilities Commission. They had meant to write "megawatt," of course, but instead typed "negawatt." The error was picked up by energy activist Amory Lovins, founder of the Rocky Mountain Institute, co-author of *Natural Capitalism*, and an advocate of what he calls "soft energy paths," which

encourage efficiency and renewable energy over traditional energy sources such as coal.

Lovins recognized the genius of the new term, and
began to refer to a "negawatt" as a watt of energy created from conservation or efficiency, which he estimates
to be a "trillion-dollar-a-year global market." He was
also able to draw attention to the fact that as a society
we were far too focused on energy generation — sink-
ing hundreds of billions of dollars into large electricity
plants that created vast amounts of pollution — when it
made more sense to focus on using the energy we have
more efficiently.

While Canada has become fixated on developing hydrocarbons, developing the negawatt represents
an even larger energy opportunity with significant
economic potential. A report by Deutsche Bank found
that investment in energy efficiency created between
two and four times more jobs than an equivalent-sized
investment in old energy. Canada is well positioned
to capture this economic opportunity. With its highly
respected educational institutions, well-informed consumers, and strong workforce, the country could be one
of the first to create the smart grid of the future.

The advent of the "smart grid" — essentially the
marriage of modern information technology with the
electricity system — is based on the premise that people

will use energy resources more efficiently if given the tools, and the price signals, to allow them to change patterns of behaviour. An important step in developing the smart grid is to move toward a "time-of-use pricing," where electricity rates would fluctuate based on demand. The natural price of energy varies depending on the time of day we use it. For example, on a hot summer business day, demand for power is likely to skyrocket with the use of air conditioning, and with it the cost of the power. Price signals can help to redistribute that power demand into the evening, and by doing so reduce the need for expensive peaking power — and the greenhouse gases and smog that accompany it. For the first time, consumers will engage with how energy is produced and consumed, and change their behaviour to use it more efficiently.

One entrepreneur who believes that a new focus on energy efficiency, time-of-use pricing, and the smart grid is on its way is Stuart Lombard. In the 1990s Lombard started one of Canada's first Internet companies, just when the Internet was taking off. A few years later, he sold that company and went on to become a venture capitalist with J. L. Albright Venture Partners, where he oversaw a number of technology investments.

In 2008 Lombard founded a company called Ecobee, whose goal was to create a device that would allow consumers to understand how they were using energy, and to shift their behaviour to begin to use it more efficiently. He imagined a time in the not-too-distant future when a much greater level of intelligence will be programmed into the energy grid of the future, allowing the user to make choices that will save them energy and money. But he felt that the devices currently available on the marketplace were difficult to program, and generally not consumer friendly. He imagined a tool that would be similar to an iPod: sleek, well designed, easy to use, and attractive. In short, he imagined using the know-how of the consumer electronics industry to usher the home energy industry into the future.

Lombard set out to design a home energy device that consumers would find easy and even fun to use. What he came up with is a full-colour, user-friendly, BlackBerry-and-computer-enabled smart thermostat that allows the user to see how much energy they are consuming, and to program it to use energy more efficiently. It's been shown that even just being aware of how you use energy is enough to cause a behavioural shift; but being able to significantly lower energy bills is a powerful motivator, and one that Lombard believes will drive demand for his product. But he is not only thinking about electricity — he anticipates a time when other resources such as water will also be at a premium. So the Ecobee has been engineered to manage water use as well. This insight is relatively unique, and may provide the Ecobee with a distinct competitive advantage in the future.

If entrepreneurs like Stuart Lombard can make smart energy choices easy for the homeowner, this will be a major breakthrough in the way we use electricity, and will give consumers a powerful new tool — one that will help them reduce their energy use and save money without compromising their comfort one iota. It will also help to complete the transformation of our energy systems from non adaptive and unintelligent one-way delivery of electrons to a much more sophisticated system that will increase efficiency in the future.

MANY OF THE TOOLS FOR BUILDING A new energy system are now available to us. We have the means to create renewable energy systems from the wind, sun, water, and earth. We also have demand management technologies, and the ability to build a smart grid. But rarely have these different capabilities been fully integrated. That's the goal of a community on Vancouver Island and an organization called First Power, which is helping First Nations communities move toward a renewable future.

Located in the rainforests of Clayoquot Sound — 20 kilometres north of the outdoor adventure mecca of

Tofino on the western side of Vancouver Island — the Hesquiaht, like many remote First Nations communities, has relied for decades on propane-generated power. Not only does this cause massive amounts of pollution, it's also incredibly expensive, costing as much as 50 cents a kilowatt per hour (many times more expensive than energy for most grid-connected communities). At this price, the small community of forty homes spends more than $250,000 a year on diesel fuel alone. But this high price for conventional energy creates an ideal opportunity to cost-effectively replace dirty energy with clean energy. It's an opportunity that people like Carol Anne Hilton do not want to miss.

Hilton is the economic development minister for the Hesquiaht. A slight woman with short brown hair, she is a driving force in the community and an advocate for the project. She believes energy independence is directly linked to greater control over a community's affairs.

"We see energy as being a perfect fit to create autonomy in our village and in our territory," she declares confidently.

To realize this vision, Hilton and the Hesquiaht have teamed up with First Power, an organization that develops renewable energy and energy autonomy for First Nations. Donna Morton, co-founder of First Power, explains that the idea is partly about First Nations communities "owning renewable energy and clean technology systems," but her ultimate goal is to use this opportunity to foster what she calls "community empowerment." Although this may sound like semantics, in practice it's a very specific strategy that places significant weight on the unique cultural identity of the communities they work in.

First Power goes to great lengths to work within the cultural context of the First Nations communities by "culturally marking" the technology through, for example, painting solar panels with local artwork and giving wind turbines the look of totem poles. Although this may sound trivial, this strategy has been shown to dramatically increase community acceptance of these new systems, reducing vandalism — which has been a problem in other First Nations communities — to virtually zero. In this respect, the experience of the Hesquiaht may have much to teach other communities that adopt renewable energy systems. For gaining community acceptance is critical to the ongoing maintenance and management of distributed renewable energy, not just on Vancouver Island but everywhere.

Leveraging the potential operating savings from eliminating diesel, First Nations and the Hesquiaht plan to raise as much as $2 million to invest in renewable energy systems in this small community. One of the exciting things about this project is that it will include a broad range of technologies, including solar thermal on every house for hot water; solar photovoltaic, wind turbines, and small hydro for electricity; aggressive demand-side management technologies; and potentially a pelletizer for wood waste — of which there is plenty in the area — for generating electricity and heat. Altogether, the Hesquiaht have the potential to create a vibrant off-grid community, marrying a wide array of technologies, the likes of which is virtually unique in Canada.

If they are successful, the Hesquiaht of Clayoquot Sound could be a model for other communities across the country. Projects like this one can help to educate other communities — Native and non-Native alike — about the best way to build renewable energy into our electricity systems in a meaningful way. If so, it may point to a profound revolution that could transform the country.

GREENING OUR ENERGY INFRASTRUCTURE is a massive project, and may come to define the twenty-first century like nothing else. Developing new power sources such as wind and solar; updating our aging electricity transmission infrastructure to deliver power efficiently;

providing the tools to consumers to be able to best manage their electricity use and the time they use it; and integrating the communications and transportation system into this new infrastructure: these are developments that will require public and private investment on an unparalleled scale. Finding the capital to invest in this wholesale renovation is critical for Canada's competitiveness, and it will drive entrepreneurial activity and create jobs.

But even if Canada is successful at making this transition, it will still address only a part of our energy challenges. We will have to contend with significant greenhouse gas emissions coming from the transportation sector. Unless we end our love affair with the car — an unlikely possibility — demand for oil is likely to continue to rise, and with it air pollution and greenhouse gas emissions. The only other alternative is to develop a truly green car. While this prospect seems a monumental challenge, it is also an economic opportunity of staggering proportions. And for a country that relies so heavily on the automotive sector for jobs, it's a critical component of our future competitiveness and economic health.

Chapter Four

WHO REVIVED THE ELECTRIC CAR?

IN THE SUMMER OF 1988 AND 1989 I worked out of a small camp north of Lake Superior. I was tree planting again, this time in Ontario. And although by now I was making a reliable income, the work was no easier than it had been in British Columbia. We were based out of a small community called Kashabowie, which was not much more than a few homes (and, amazingly, a beer store!) scattered along the Trans-Canada Highway. We stayed in small trailers parked beside a motel along the highway, and at night you could hear the occasional car swish by. I would sit in bed and imagine where they might be travelling to. If they were heading west, I wondered if they were on their way to Manitoba or maybe all the way to British Columbia; if they were going east, perhaps it was Montreal, Fredericton, or Cape Breton.

Being stuck on the side of the Trans-Canada Highway is like going hungry with a plate of food just out of reach. I could taste the freedom of the highway as the cars zoomed past, and visualized the country, stretched along that long, clean line of asphalt. If there was anywhere you wanted to go in Canada, you could set off from here. The country was defined by that road, which tied together all of our regional and linguistic differences like a necklace.

If the railways defined our economies and our country in the nineteenth century, surely it was the highway that defined them in the twentieth century. Although this statement is frequently made about the United States, it seems to me that it is equally true of Canada. Indeed, the origins of the car industry in Canada date back to the year of confederation, 1867, when Henry Seth Taylor of Stanstead, Quebec, built the first horseless carriage. Stanstead's steam-powered buggy had a maximum speed of 24 kilometres per hour, but suffered from a significant design oversight: no brakes.

The automotive industry really got going in the early part of the twentieth century, when the Ford Motor Company of Canada was established in 1904, only a year after Henry Ford began manufacturing cars. Windsor, Ontario — located across the river from Detroit, the mecca of the world's automotive industry — became the capital of the Canadian auto sector. By 1918, Canada was the second largest auto manufacturer in the world.

Canada has maintained its position as a leader in car production throughout the twentieth century. The single most important factor for this was the 1965 Canada–U.S. Automotive Products Trade Agreement (Auto Pact), which reduced tariffs on American cars coming into Canada, but in return guaranteed manufacturing capacity for Canada. Since then, Canada's automotive industry has continued to grow, and as recently as 2006 the industry accounted for 24 percent of manufacturing trade in Canada, shipping more than $80 billion worth of cars and car parts, and accounting for 158,000 jobs. It is by far the largest manufacturing industry in Canada. In a sense, then, the automotive sector runs contrary to Harold Innis's staples theory, which posited that Canadians are merely "hewers of wood and drawers of water."

Despite these impressive numbers, the Canadian automotive industry has for some time been vulnerable. For one, Canadian manufacturing plants tended to build larger, inefficient cars and SUVs, which were potentially vulnerable to higher energy prices. And though Canada punched above its weight in car assembly, much of the research and development was done in head offices in the U.S. and overseas. Worse still, Canadian automotive companies were merely American branch plant subsidiaries, and so lacked any decision-making authority. Even the Canadian–owned parts manufacturers were often reliant on the American companies for the lion's share of their business.

Other structural economic problems, such as labour costs, created major problems for the industry when countries such as Mexico and Brazil began establishing themselves as dynamic new players in the global automotive business. As a result, the industry depended on a low Canadian dollar, an economic advantage that has not lasted.

By 2007, American car manufacturers were running into some major headwinds, which had a direct impact on the Canadian branch plants. A principal cause of their troubles was the climbing cost of gasoline, which undermined the most profitable part of the American auto business. While companies such as Toyota and Honda were building smaller, more fuel-efficient cars, American automakers were innovating in the wrong direction, building ever larger, more powerful gas guzzlers. Later, it became clear that the American car industry's lobbying efforts had come back to bite them.

After years of vigorously resisting any increases in fuel efficiency standards, the U.S. auto industry was not prepared to compete with foreign manufacturers whose jurisdictions maintained higher mileage standards. The American auto industry relied instead on the extravagant profit margins of the large SUVs. So when the price of energy spiked in 2008, the large car market collapsed.

In 2008, the global financial crisis compounded the problems, driving consumers out of the car market. In Canada the numbers were dire. Revenues plunged from almost $70 billion in 2004 and 2005 to slightly more than $30 billion in 2009. In the U.S., the financial losses were so steep that the auto industry required massive restructuring and significant government bailouts. Both the Canadian and Ontario governments announced investments of $4 billion to keep General Motors and Chrysler afloat. And there were unprecedented job losses across North America when factories were forced to curtail or shut down their operations.

The American car companies — and the Canadian automotive industry by extension — had fallen behind, and were unequipped to fulfill the demands of the market. But their short-sighted resistance to higher mileage standards was only part of the problem. Large American car companies — GM, Ford, and Chrysler — had also bet on the wrong technology. Over the previous ten years these automakers had invested heavily in hydrogen fuel cells. But the challenges of developing cars driven by fuel cells proved to be more difficult than expected, and companies such as Burnaby, B.C.–based Ballard Power Systems struggled to reduce the costs of manufacturing hydrogen-powered engines. It seemed that the fuel cell industry was perpetually five years away from developing a commercially available car.

More challenging still was building the extensive infrastructure required to handle, store, and distribute hydrogen to service a fleet of cars. While struggling with these technical and structural impediments, the fuel cell industry faced growing skepticism that it could even deliver meaningful environmental gains. Originally the fuel cell was positioned as a magic, emissions-free technology; you could drive a car and produce only water vapour. But hydrogen still had to be produced, and it required energy to do so.

While hydrogen fuel cells fought to find a real purchasing place in the car industry, electricity was gaining traction. It was certainly less of a technical challenge: the technology for electric cars was readily available, and the electricity infrastructure ubiquitous. There was an important historical precedent as well; in the early part of the twentieth century, many cars were powered using electricity. But with the discovery of cheap and plentiful oil, the promise of electric cars was never fully realized, and since then efforts to revive the electric car have largely failed. The ill-fated General Motors EV1 — which was the subject of the documentary film *Who Killed the Electric Car?* — was the most public example of a failed experiment in electricity. But the market shifted significantly with the advent of hybrid cars, originally produced by Toyota and Honda. The commercial success of hybrids opened up a new path for the automotive industry, reviving the idea of the electric car.

IN 2007 I WITNESSED THE TRANSFORMATION of the car industry. I must admit, I didn't know it at the time. All I saw was the proverbial two guys in a garage. And in this case it was *literally* two guys in a garage in Concord, Ontario. The two guys were Ricardo Bazzarella and Akos Toth. And the garage was where they were developing their plug-in hybrid technologies.

Bazzarella and Toth had met at Hydrogenics, a leading fuel cell company, where they helped to develop fuel cell technologies for cars. With engineering degrees from the University of Waterloo and the University of Toronto, respectively, Bazzarella and Toth came to the realization that the future of the automotive industry lay not in hydrogen fuel cells, but rather in hybrid fuel systems.

They left their comfortable jobs at Hydrogenics to start a new company called Hymotion, which provided the means for hybrids to plug into the electricity grid. This concept inverted the emphasis of the hybrid engine.

The original design of the hybrid emphasized its self-reliance. It did not need to be plugged into the electricity grid, which meant that it drove and operated like any car. Using features such as regenerative braking, the electric engine was able to recapture electricity and to support the gas engine. But, in essence, the internal combustion engine was still doing the lion's share of the work.

By adding a new lithium-ion battery that could be charged through an extension cord and a regular 120-volt outlet, Hymotion's plug-in hybrids were now more like electric cars that had a gas engine as a backup for longer voyages. In fact, the vehicle could travel up to 50 kilometres almost entirely on electric power. Since most people drive less than 50 kilometres a day, Hymotion had effectively created one of the first highly functional electric cars.

Not only was their new car significantly more fuel efficient than any other on the market, but it could drive just as far, just as fast, with the added benefit of reducing greenhouse gas emissions and local air pollution. Although the environmental benefits vary depending on how electricity is generated, plug-in hybrids can deliver greenhouse gas emissions reductions even if the electricity is derived from dirty coal-fired power plants. This is especially true if the electric battery is recharged during off-peak hours.

The founders of Hymotion had a big idea but limited financing to see it through. So they had to bootstrap their business and find an application for their new technology that could produce revenues quickly. They started to offer plug-in retrofits that would outfit a standard Toyota Prius. The new rechargeable battery was installed into the spare tire well, taking up no trunk space. Although the price was high — $9,000 per car — there were cost savings, too, as the expense of running in electric mode was substantially cheaper than the cost of gasoline. The company managed to generate revenues of $120,000 in their first year.

When I visited them in 2006, Bazzarella and Toth took me for a drive in their car. Being a Prius driver, I am accustomed to hearing the engine move back and forth between electric and gasoline. The Hymotion, however, remained continuously in the electric mode. For all intents and purposes Bazzarella and Toth had created a fully functional electric car in a small garage in Concord, Ontario — something the enormous global auto industry with its billions of dollars in research and development had not yet succeeded in doing.

We chatted afterwards and discussed their options to grow the company. They were considering raising investment capital, and had taken on a U.S.–based partner to manage fundraising. By 2007, Hymotion came one step closer to realizing their dream of creating an electric car. They sold the company to A123 Systems, a leading developer of lithium-ion batteries — their supplier of choice, and another company that is critical to the reinvention of our transportation industry and infrastructure.

A123 IS AT THE FOREFRONT OF developing the next generation of battery technology. Reducing battery weight and decreasing charge times would fundamentally revolutionize the automotive industry, and dramatically increase the market potential of electric cars. Lithium-ion batteries like those developed by A123 Systems are potentially a step in the right direction. With a long life and good energy characteristics, they are also significantly lighter than the nickel metal hydride (NiMH) batteries that are the standard in today's hybrid cars. Even so, the weight-to-storage ratio of lithium-ion batteries means they have a long way to go before they can put the internal combustion engine out of business.

One of the people who may be close to seeing a major breakthrough in battery storage is Ian Clifford, CEO of

Zenn Motor Company. Clifford's interest in electric cars started when he tried to buy one for himself. He looked at all of the options, including the EV1, but could not find anything he actually wanted to purchase and drive home until he managed to get his hands on one of two hundred 1959 Renault Dauphines that had been rebuilt as electric cars. It had about 6,400 kilometres on it, went almost 100 kilometres an hour, and had a 100-kilometre range on a lead-acid battery. He happily drove his new vehicle around Toronto, attracting attention wherever he went. When the car broke down, he called the manufacturer and asked where he could get a 1959 electric Renault Dauphine fixed. He was told to look in the phone directory under "lift trucks." Clifford then realized that there were thousands of functioning electric vehicles — they just weren't cars.

In 2000 Clifford sold his Internet marketing company and began to consider his next career move. His electric Dauphin was still getting attention wherever he went, and he knew there was an untapped market. So he decided to start a company that would market and sell electric cars. He called the company Feel Good Cars. At first he began buying all the Renault Dauphines he could get his hands on and converting them to electric. By 2002 he realized that it would be less capital intensive to enter the low-speed vehicle market. So he designed the Zenn: an electric car suitable for urban areas with a top speed of 40 kilometres per hour.

At the time I lived around the corner from Ian in Toronto's Annex neighbourhood. I remember my wife telling me one day that a guy down the street was building an electric car and that I should go visit him. So one day, I dropped by to have a chat. The Zenn was parked out front, and my first impression was that the vehicle looked like a big toy. Half the size of a regular compact car and powered completely by electric batteries, it was the first car I had seen designed specifically for the urban environment.

Clifford met me at the door, dressed casually in jeans. We sat in his dining room, where he told me about his plan to develop the Zenn. I was amazed that anyone would have the chutzpah to start a car company. It seemed like a hugely ambitious plan, competing against global companies with billions of dollars to invest in product development and marketing. But Clifford had a powerful insight; he foresaw that the car industry would have to move toward electrification before many others did, and certainly before those running the large car companies realized it.

Ian Clifford believed that what was needed to make an electric car truly mainstream was new battery technology. So he set out to find a better battery that would transform the automotive market. He spent years meeting with developers, and eventually stumbled onto the founders of a company called EEstor. Unlike most of the technologies he'd seen, the EEstor battery was not promising incremental change but rather a quantum leap forward, with power densities potentially three to four times greater than anything else on the market, along with significant weight reductions, increased potential longevity, and reduced manufacturing costs. But the company was still in start-up mode; Ian describes the operation as essentially being "two guys and a lawyer." They had not been successful in raising capital to develop the company, but he thought he could help make that happen.

In 2005, Clifford agreed to buy an exclusive licence for the EEstor battery for vehicles weighing more than 14 kilos. EEstor went on to raise money from leading Silicon Valley venture capital firm Kleiner Perkins. After Feel Good Cars went public in 2006, and changed its name to the Zenn Motor Company, the company invested another $10 million to buy an ownership stake in EEstor, giving Zenn a significant equity interest. EEstor still has to prove its viability in the marketplace, and Clifford is expecting their first commercial prototypes in 2010. But if it does work out, as Clifford believes it will, EEstor will revolutionize the automotive sector, helping electric cars become a reality.

WHILE THE WORLD WAITS FOR A better battery, the electric
car industry is still moving forward. Perhaps the most
ingenious innovation — which is not a technological
innovation at all, but potentially groundbreaking none-
theless — is being advanced by Shai Agassi, an Israeli
software engineer and entrepreneur turned global
visionary. Aside from being young, handsome, and rich
— he sold his last company for $400 million — he is
high on charisma and smarts.

Agassi stumbled onto a radical idea that might just
turn the automotive industry on its head. If the electric
car was being held back by the technology of batteries
that were so heavy and so slow to charge, could you create
an infrastructure that would compensate for this problem
in some other way? Agassi began to consider the idea of
creating electric fuelling stations, which would be mod-
elled after gas stations for conventional cars. But instead
of recharging the battery, which would take too much
time for most people, Agassi imagined a robotic arm that
would literally take the battery out of your car and replace
it with a fully charged battery in a process that would be
as quick as filling a tank of gas. Your old battery would
then be recharged and placed in another car.

If you could build enough of these stations in a
geographic area, Agassi reasoned, the other limitations
of the electric car would be less of a problem. If a driver

exceeded the range of the battery, he or she could simply pull into a service station and get a new one put in. Even more enticing, under Agassi's model the car owner doesn't own the battery, but just pays for the electricity to use it. Because the battery is the most expensive part of an electric car, the purchase price of the vehicle would drop dramatically. And because electricity is generally much more cost effective than gas for transportation, theoretically the consumer would also enjoy long-term savings.

Agassi named his company Better Place after he attended the 2005 World Economic Forum, which asked the question: "How do you make the world a better place by 2020?" Agassi thought he knew the answer: by making the world less reliant on fossil fuels by developing zero-emissions vehicles powered by renewable energy. It's a strong vision that animates the goals of the company still. But making the world less reliant on oil also carries with it inevitable political overtones. In fact, Agassi first outlined his vision for Better Place at a conference on the Middle East attended by the likes of former U.S. president Bill Clinton and Israeli prime minister Shimon Peres.

To launch the company Shai Agassi invested his own capital, and then raised significant financing from investors such as VantagePoint and Morgan Stanley. In 2009 he unveiled the automated "battery swap stations."

He also engaged car manufacturers in discussions about creating a more consistent car design to meet his battery stations' specifications, which led to the announcement of a partnership with Nissan–Renault. And Better Place has since announced a number of locations where it would test its infrastructure, including Israel, Denmark, Australia, and more recently Ontario.

Critics contend that Better Place will not be able to convince enough car manufacturers to build vehicles to its specifications, which would limit the kinds of cars the stations can service and future growth in other markets. And they will face significant competition from new car companies such as Tesla, which are following a more conventional model for electric cars that do not require battery swaps. But if Better Place can overcome these hurdles, it may be the company that makes the electric car mainstream.

HOWEVER IT HAPPENS — be it through plug-in hybrids, new and more powerful car batteries, or Better Place's battery swap stations — if electric cars become a reality they will open up the door to a number of interesting energy innovations that are likely to extend far beyond the transportation sector. For one, there is the possibility for significant emissions reductions since electric vehicles — even when the electricity comes from dirty sources like coal — operate at efficiencies of as much as 90 percent, whereas an internal combustion engine is closer to 20 percent. But electric cars may also play a critical role in the development of the electricity grid. Because many sources of renewable energy are intermittent, power is often unavailable at peak hours. Wind is often blowing at night, for example, when power demand is lowest. Today, if the demand for electricity is not concurrent with the time the energy is created, power is simply lost.

The flip side of this conundrum is that because renewable energies cannot provide consistent power, they cannot be relied upon for base-load generation. But a fleet of electric cars can help to store a consistent supply of renewable energy to meet demand. Essentially, we can store energy when it is plentiful and cheap, then release it as required. Cars will then become giant batteries for a grid reoriented around renewable energy.

Imagine for a moment how this might change the way we use our cars in the future. Picture a day, ten years from now. When you climb into your car in the morning, a monitor on the dashboard informs you that the battery has been fully charged with energy provided from wind power generators running through the night. You drive to work, where you park in your regular spot, and your car battery is automatically connected to an electricity terminal, which will ensure that it is charged throughout the day. During the hours of peak electricity use, the terminal may also provide a prompt on your BlackBerry, asking you if you would like to sell the excess electricity from your car back to the grid at an attractive price. You press "Agree," and your car battery supplies power to the grid.

Integrating a car's battery with the electricity grid in this way will mitigate our reliance on expensive and polluting energy sources. It will also drive a very new relationship among our electricity grid, our communications infrastructure, and our cars. These three enormous global industries will be integrated into one continuous energy web — a new smart grid — that will optimize our use of valuable energy resources, while offering tremendous economic opportunities.

THE TRANSFORMATION OF THE automotive sector is an event we cannot afford to miss. There will be significant innovations in all aspects of how we make cars. And for provinces such as Ontario, whose economy is reliant on the car manufacturing sector, it may be a necessity to compete in the long term. But the reality is that an automotive fleet powered entirely by electricity is still many years away. So for the foreseeable future the internal combustion engine will remain dominant. And while it is, the world's "addiction to oil" — in the words of George W. Bush — will continue. This means that Canada will have to reconcile itself with the uncomfortable luck of being home to one of the world's largest energy deposits, the Athabasca tar sands.

Chapter Five

AN ENERGY SUPERPOWER

I'M 300 METRES IN THE AIR looking down at an open-pit mine that stretches for perhaps a kilometre, maybe more. Giant trucks crawl across the surface, carrying loads of black bitumen and lined up like worker ants on a giant anthill. On one side are two enormous tailing ponds, though in scale they are much closer to lakes than ponds. On the other side is an enormous processing plant and refinery, where flares burn and a huge smokestack belches out a thick, grey plume of smoke. Surprisingly close to the refinery is the Athabasca River; even from this distance its murky brown colour is slightly alarming.

"What's the water like down there?" one of the other passengers in the helicopter asks the pilot over his speakerphone.

"You wouldn't want to eat the fish," is his laconic reply.

We let it go at that.

Across the tundra one can see a number of such operations, the open-pit mines of the oil sands, where the bitumen comes close enough to the surface that the best means of accessing it is to pull off the top layer of soil — the "overburden," as it's called — that exposes the dark layer of bitumen-saturated earth beneath. The process is inherently invasive, as huge swaths of tundra are torn up. It's also fundamentally inefficient. We have come a long way from those gushers in the desert that gave rise to the Age of Oil in the twentieth century, where a single hole dug in the desert ground would release gobs of flowing crude. Now we are forced to strip off 20 metres of topsoil to excavate the bitumen-soaked layer below. And this soil requires further refining to separate the bitumen from the rocks, sand, and water, and from there it requires even more processing to become synthetic crude.

As we pass over the Suncor operation the pilot reminds us that the entire area beneath has been licensed for mining. Hundreds of kilometres of pristine tundra are laced with drills that are testing the geology of the soil. We fly over a number of such operations, and in each case it's the same — vast tracks of open-pit mining, huge tailing ponds, and enormous processing facilities — until we come to one that's a little different. The factory looks the same, but there is no open pit and from the helicopter it also looks less ugly.

This is what they call in situ mining, and though visually it is more pleasing and the geographical footprint has been significantly reduced, it comes with its own problems. The in situ mines were developed to access the bitumen that is too far below the surface to justify open-pit mining. Instead they use a process called steam-assisted gravity drainage (SAGD): a pipe directs steam into the bitumen layer below the surface and heats the bitumen to a point where it becomes liquid, then another pipe sucks it out like a straw. While this process results in less damage to the earth's surface, it is even more energy-intensive.

On the ground you get a different but complementary picture of this process. As we tour the Suncor facility, our guide goes to great efforts to convince us of the seriousness with which the company takes its environmental responsibility. When we stop by one of the tailing ponds, the guide discusses the company's plans to reclaim this pond by removing the water and slag and eventually returning it to its original state. It becomes clear, though, that this has yet to happen anywhere in the oil sands — no tailing ponds have been fully reclaimed despite the fact that some are more than forty years old. But the company wants very badly to convince us — and perhaps themselves — that they are operating in an environmentally responsible manner.

The facility is liberally adorned with communications messages to this effect. Computer terminals tout the company's efforts to reduce greenhouse gas emissions and to go beyond all requirements and expectations to manage their environmental footprint. I suspect that at some level their intentions are good, and in fairness Suncor is considered one of the most environmentally progressive oil sands operators, and have a genuine interest in making its operations more sustainable. Which is perhaps why they allowed us to tour their operation; undoubtedly many other oil sands operators care a great deal less about the environment and are not likely keen to offer tours to suspected environmentalists.

And yet, as a visitor, you cannot help but notice the contradiction between this environmental message and the fundamental reality of this dirty business, the signs of which are pretty much everywhere you look. Take the trucks, for example. I walked into the truck repair shop, and at first I couldn't see any trucks at all. Not because they weren't there, but rather because I was looking in the wrong direction. I was looking straight ahead, when really I needed to look up — way up — for all around me were trucks. But they were so large I had mistaken them for buildings. That's when I learned about the 797, the world's largest truck.

With its barrel open, the 797 stands 50 feet tall. The driver sits 21 feet off the ground and must climb a ladder to get to his cab. The six wheels are 12 feet tall, and cost $60,000 each. Each 797 can carry 450 tons of raw ore, and uses 6,800 litres of gas per filling. At $5.5 million a pop, these trucks are a physical manifestation of the scale of the operation — how much energy, matter, debris, and resources we're dealing with here.

One of the buildings we visit is the technological control centre for the entire project, something akin to the bridge from the *Starship Enterprise* in *Star Trek*. On the huge computer screens that encircle the room you can see all stages of the operation. After the truck deposits its 450-ton load into an open grate, the debris is sent through two enormous rotating jaws which crush everything into pieces about 45 centimetres or less. Huge boulders and rocks are smashed and crunched down to the size of a football. The materials are then injected with a slurry of hot water, and the bitumen is separated from the non-bituminous parts of the stream — the rocks, for example. Once it is isolated, the bitumen is sent to the refiner. But the inefficiency of the process is apparent in the numbers — a ton of raw material is required to create roughly a barrel of bitumen, which results in a half barrel of crude. And a lot of energy and a lot of waste are created on the way.

I leave the plant trying to mentally reconcile the idea that companies like Suncor — and some of the other oil sands operators — are trying to do everything they can to create a sustainable process. But the undeniable impression I'm left with is that the process seems fundamentally unsustainable. Perhaps both are true: these companies are trying to operate responsibly within a process that is inefficient on a massive scale. But who's to blame? Is it right to condemn the companies and their employees and executives? Is it right for me, an energy consumer of historically unparalleled levels, to condemn them? Perhaps their efforts to convince me otherwise are a cry for respect, for understanding. For who are they producing this oil for, if not me?

George Poitras has a unique perspective on the sustainability of the oil sands. He is an industry relations representative and former band chief for the Fort Chipewyan Cree who live on the shores of Lake Athabasca. His story is a sad one, but he tells it with exceptional intelligence, and I must say with incredible fairness and equanimity. Over the last ten years or so —

as the oil sands projects have grown in number and scale
— Poitras's community has suffered. It began with the
discovery of high levels of cancer, including very rare
cancers, in many of the Fort Chipewyan Cree.

Finally the local physician, Dr. John O'Connor, went
public with his concerns. Instead of conducting a proper
investigation into his allegations, Health Canada brought
a formal complaint against O'Connor for causing undue
alarm. Despite all of this, he remains highly regarded
in Fort Chipewyan for having the courage to challenge
the powers that be and protect his community. And due
to his public pronouncements, the community started
to receive some media attention and support from environmental non-governmental organizations (ENGOs).

Poitras believes that the high rates of cancer in his
community are linked to toxins in the fish and animals
that still represent most people's diet. Indeed, strange
deformities in the wildlife are frequently reported.
When I was there, for example, they had recently caught
a fish with two mouths.

The Chipewyan Cree have intervened on a number
of applications for oil sands licences, but their concerns
have never been addressed. In fact, no application for
an oil sands licence has ever been turned down, even
though the Fort Chipewyan Cree have actively opposed
a number of projects. Further, Poitras believes that the

overseeing bodies really only represent the views of industry, and have no concern for local stakeholders such as the Chipewyan Cree. Poitras claims that the government is not honouring its obligation to consult with First Nations, an obligation that according to Poitras is enshrined in the 1982 Constitution Act.

In 2008 the Chipewyan Cree dropped out of the Cumulative Environmental Management Association (CEMA), a "multi-stakeholder" group established by the Alberta government to "study the cumulative environmental effects of industrial development in the region and produce guidelines and management frameworks." They were followed by three environmental organizations, including the Toxics Watch Society of Alberta and the Pembina Institute.

"Frankly speaking, we can no longer legitimize a process that both the oil sands industry and government have been using as a shield to deflect criticism about the cumulative environmental impacts of oil sands development," said Myles Kitagawa, a director with the Toxics Watch Society. Their principal recommendation was a moratorium on new licences for the oil sands until a more functional and legitimate environmental process had been established. This idea has attracted a wide constituency, and has been supported by prominent and highly regarded Albertans such as Peter Lougheed.

But the Alberta government shows little signs of stopping, or even slowing down, the issuance of new licences. And the federal government has no stomach for intruding on an area of provincial jurisdiction. And the business community continues to support the oil sands, investing large sums in these gargantuan energy reserves. In fact, our pilot informs us that the previous day, Bill Gates and Warren Buffett had flown in the very same helicopter to take their own tour of the area.

NOTHING WAS MORE IMPORTANT TO the development of the twentieth century than the discovery of cheap, plentiful oil. For a time, that energy seemed virtually unlimited, and it left no part of our culture untouched. From the highways which spread in all directions, connecting the great cities and suburbs to one another; to the industrialization of food, which was powered by synthetic fertilizer, petroleum's first cousin; to our industrial and manufacturing sectors, which grew reliant on cheap energy — these modern developments were built around easily accessible reservoirs of oil that flowed from the ground with very little coaxing.

But in 1956, M. King Hubbert, a geophysicist who worked for Shell, realized that this energy boom might not last forever. Hubbert noticed that oil and gas production followed a natural bell curve — since termed the Hubbert curve. He went so far as to predict that the U.S. would reach its peak production around 1970. Hubbert was roundly ridiculed; experts in the field argued that his projections were wildly pessimistic and that production in the U.S. would continue to grow. But in 1970, U.S. oil production did in fact peak, and Hubbert's theory proved true.

Hubbert made another important prediction: that the world's oil production would peak some time between 2004 and 2008. Again, conventional wisdom was set against him. Even if the American reservoirs had been depleted, other energy resources would be discovered. But the concept of "peak oil" had given rise to an ongoing debate as to when the world's oil production would in fact begin to decline. Some have gone beyond rhetoric and invested substantial sums betting that peak oil has already happened, and that energy prices will inexorably rise going forward. One notable proponent of that view is the iconoclastic fund manager Eric Sprott, one of Canada's most successful investors.

Perhaps the ultimate question is not so much whether world oil production has peaked, but rather whether we have seen the end of easily accessible energy. In the end this is the bigger issue. Whether we have technically seen the peak production of oil — whether that happened last night, or whether it will happen in twenty years — is largely academic, highly technical, and fundamentally unknowable; you're not likely to know if peak oil has happened until well after it has occurred. But whether we have hit peak oil or not, it is becoming increasingly clear that energy is getting harder to find and to develop. And this, in the end, is more relevant to our lives.

A good way to think about this issue is in the context of energy return on energy invested, or EROI. The concept is simple, and highly useful. EROI measures how many units of energy input is required for every unit of energy output. Many of the original oil reserves that were tapped in the early part of the twentieth century provided an exceptional EROI of 25 to 1. In other words, for every unit of energy input we were able to extract 25 units of energy.

But most of the low-hanging fruit was used up in the twentieth century, and now we've moved on to energy sources that are more difficult to extract and have a lower EROI. The Athabasca oil sands have an EROI in the neighbourhood of 1 to 4. That is, for every unit of energy we put in we get only four units out. In other words, the oil sands are approximately six times less efficient than the easily accessible oil reserves tapped in the twentieth century.

EROI analyzes the virtues of different forms of energy beyond economics. Another advantage is that it contains within it a notion of the externalities inherent in energy production, particularly climate considerations. For example, an energy source with a much lower EROI generally emits more greenhouse gases per unit of energy. And so we get a glimpse of the challenges we may face in the future; as EROI diminishes, more of our energy will be utilized in developing energy, and each unit of that energy will be more polluting.

THE SCALE OF ENVIRONMENTAL problems associated with the oil sands demands attention. The implications for Canada's greenhouse gas emissions are staggering. The National Energy Board estimates that oil sands production uses 21 million cubic metres of natural gas per day, and that this number will rise to 61 million cubic metres per day. It is expected that the oil sands could account for as much as 50 percent of all of the natural gas use in Western Canada. And, in all likelihood, much of the natural gas that is projected to come down the Mackenzie Valley Pipeline will be used to develop the oil sands. Considering that natural gas is a relatively clean-burning fuel, using it to produce energy from the oil sands is likened by many environmentalists to turning gold into lead.

The oil sands' intense energy needs are wreaking havoc on Canada's efforts to curtail emissions. In fact, according to a report from the Pembina Institute, the oil sands are expected to account for 47 percent of the increase in greenhouse gas emissions in Canada between 2003 and 2010. And according to the OECD's 2008 Economic Survey on Canada, emissions from the oil sands are projected to grow from 29 megatonnes a year in 2006 to 108 megatonnes by 2020; that's a mind-blowing 271-percent increase over a period in which Canada hopes to decrease emissions by 20 percent. In short, Canada cannot hope to achieve its goals of reducing greenhouse gas emissions without addressing the inexorable rise in emissions that are coming from the oil sands.

Unless there is a major focus on reducing greenhouse gas emissions, and water and energy use, this project will continue to be a black eye for Canada and a danger to the environment. But cleaning up the oil sands also provides a unique opportunity. Because of the enormous size of this resource — and the environmental constraints that will inevitably be placed on it — it can become a unique testing ground for new technologies. And if successful, these technologies may also be applicable to other large fossil fuel projects worldwide.

A growing number of oil sands companies now seem to agree that further action needs to be taken to reduce their environmental footprint. For the first time ever, a group of six major oil companies — including Suncor, ConocoPhillips, and Total — are coming together under the name of the Oil Sands Leadership Initiative (OSLI) to promote and develop more sustainable practices for the industry. Because these corporations understand that their social licence to operate will come under increasing scrutiny, OSLI is an effort by the industry to reform itself from within.

The group has been intentionally quiet to start, knowing that attracting any publicity before having achieved concrete results is likely to be seen as proof that the effort is only a public relations stunt. But working groups, which include high-level senior executives from each of the participating companies, have been meeting on a range of issues that include reducing greenhouse gas emissions, and increasing energy and water efficiency. Although it's still early, groups like the Pembina Institute — an oil sands watchdog — believes it's an important first step. "They should have done it ten years ago," says Marlo Reynolds, executive director of Pembina.

The development of OSLI may help to provide a truce between some of the more progressive oil sands companies and pragmatic groups in the environmental industry. This effort to compromise may in turn help to move the discussion on to the crucial issue of technology development. The only way to reduce the environmental impact of this project — short of shutting down the oil sands, which even most critics of the industry admit is not likely to happen — will come through the development of new sustainable technology.

LIONEL KAMBEITZ THINKS HE CAN help make this happen. A gregarious and jovial environmental entrepreneur hailing from Regina, Saskatchewan, Kambeitz is the founder of HTC Purenergy, a world-leading company in the growing field of carbon capture and storage (CCS) technology. The technology works by injecting CO_2 emissions back into the ground and thus keeping it from entering the atmosphere.

In theory, the potential for CCS is impressive; it's estimated that, worldwide, CCS could store 2 trillion to 10 trillion tons of CO_2. To put that in perspective, world CO_2 output in 2004 was around 27 billion metric tons. In other words, CCS is potentially large enough to contain all of the world's CO_2 output for between 100 and 1,000 years. The other benefit of CCS is that energy companies are already using CO_2 streams for what is called "enhanced oil recovery," by injecting CO_2 into old oil wells to increase production. For example, every year

750,000 tons of CO_2 are captured at a coal gasification plant in North Dakota and delivered by pipeline to oil fields in Weyburn, Saskatchewan, operated by Calgary–based energy giant EnCana. Companies such as HTC Purenergy are developing ways to separate the CO_2 into a pure stream, to transport it, to use it for enhanced recovery of oil, and, increasingly, to make sure the CO_2 remains sequestered in the ground.

Located at the University of Regina, HTC Purenergy developed out of two affiliated programs at the university: the Greenhouse Gas Technology Centre, a facility that launched in 2001 with funding from Natural Resources Canada, and the International Test Centre for Carbon Dioxide Capture (ITC), whose mission is to develop more effective CO_2 separation processes. The HTC technology was largely developed by two notable ITC professors: Paitoon Tontiwachwuthikul, a leading expert in carbon capture and storage research, and Malcolm Wilson, a contributor to the Intergovernmental Panel on Climate Change (IPCC). Both of them have been involved in carbon capture for many years, and were instrumental in designing a CO_2-based oil recovery system for EnCana that has now been in operation for eight years.

HTC's technology allows CO_2 to be captured from the exhaust streams of large power producers. The CO_2

can then be used to encourage production in depleted oil wells, as in the EnCana case, or it can be stored underground in geologic formations. HTC believes it can significantly reduce the amount of energy required to capture CO_2, thus reducing the cost of the process.

But HTC might have remained a technology theory, lost in a laboratory at the University of Regina, had it not been discovered by Lionel Kambeitz. A serial entrepreneur with a background in environmental businesses, Kambeitz's prior company was the largest paper recycling vacuum moulding company in North America, which turned old newspapers into 55 percent of the egg flats used in North America. In 1997, after he sold the recycling business, Kambeitz bumped into his federal MP, Ralph Goodale, at the YMCA in Regina. Goodale told Kambeitz about all of the "good stuff" coming out of the University of Regina, and convinced him to take a closer look to see if anything could be commercialized. Not long afterward, Goodale hosted a meeting with the president of the university, who introduced Kambeitz to the HTC technology.

Kambeitz quickly realized the potential for CCS in the market. He discovered that in the U.S. alone CO_2 could be used to recover as much as 43 billion barrels of oil. Looking further into the future, Kambeitz could see there was potentially an even larger market in the sequestration of CO_2 to minimize climate change. So he licensed the technology from the University of Regina and set out to build HTC Purenergy.

Under Kambeitz, the company has become a leader in its field. They recently signed a licensing agreement with London–based Doosan Babcock, a global manufacturer of power plants, which included a $10 million investment in HTC. And they have spec'd out more than forty-two projects worldwide, including a $1.4 billion project to capture CO_2 from a coal plant owned by SaskPower. If HTC can succeed in building a business in CCS, it will open up a potentially vast market for other Canadian companies. It will also be a powerful example of how universities and the private sector can work together to commercialize technology in Canada.

Because of companies like HTC Purenergy and facilities like those found at the University of Regina, Saskatchewan is attracting worldwide attention as a leader in carbon capture. In September 2009, Premier Brad Wall welcomed a delegation of U.S. politicians, including senators Lindsey Graham (Republican – South Carolina) and Kay Hagan (Democrat – North Carolina), and Jessica Maher, the associate director for Congressional affairs at the White House Council of Environmental Quality. A tour of the International Test Centre for CO_2 Capture prompted Senator Graham to say, "What's [being done] in Saskatchewan is pretty good evidence that carbon sequestration not only is doable but affordable and practical."

Although the opportunities are numerous, companies such as HTC Purenergy still face challenges to implementing a CCS system. The first is cost. No one seems to have fully grappled with the additional expense of properly sequestering CO_2 from a project the size of the oil sands, but it will certainly require an investment of billions of dollars. Even using Kambeitz's cost estimation of between \$25 and \$80 per tonne of CO_2 may prove to be a real impediment to moving forward. If the cost of CCS were to be incorporated into the price of crude from the oil sands, the economics might become uncommercial (especially while the price of oil remained low). If that were the case, CCS could kill the oil sands or burden governments under a pile of debt.

Another technical question is whether CCS technology will even work in the oil sands. Because the emissions from the mining projects tend to be diffuse, it may be difficult to capture CO_2 as effectively as we can from a coal-fired power plant, for example. If we can't capture enough CO_2 then of course CCS won't work very well.

Kambeitz insists that CCS is well suited to the in situ operations because most of the emissions come from natural gas boilers and so could theoretically be captured. And he is enthusiastic about the prospect of using the captured carbon in the oil sands. If CO_2 can be used to enhance the recovery of heavy oil from the oil sands, while simultaneously sequestering the carbon permanently underground, it could be a breakthrough for the industry. But even if it can't be used on-site, CO_2 could be sent by pipeline to the oil fields of southern Alberta for enhanced recovery of conventional oil fields.

The final question is whether CO_2 will remain sequestered. If it doesn't, then the efforts (and energy) required to implement the CCS process would be wasted. But an IPCC report suggests that more than 99 percent of CO_2 is likely to be retained for over a thousand years. If this is the case, then oil corporations will likely be forced to consider using CCS technology, even if it is expensive. And if that happens, Lionel Kambeitz will be ready.

ONE MUST GUARD AGAINST being a Pollyanna with an unproven technology like CCS, but if it does prove viable it offers the federal government and Alberta's provincial government the opportunity to work together for mutual benefit, and to escape the zero-sum political game that has framed our discussions of the oil sands in the past. Building a CCS infrastructure in Alberta would incur considerable expense, but it could be a good investment for the country, one that has truly global potential.

Indeed, some of the challenges to CCS technology may ease over time. The need for sequestration could be reduced if we find other beneficial uses of CO_2. Companies such as Scarborough, Ontario–based Pond Biofuels are developing systems to utilize carbon dioxide for the production of algae to create biofuels. Algae fertilized with CO_2 doubles its weight overnight, giving rise to the potential of using waste carbon to create new energy streams. Although the technology is still in the development phase — Pond has partnered with St. Mary's Cement to build a pilot algae farm using emissions from the cement factory — it holds promise that one day carbon dioxide emissions from the oil sands could be captured and used to create relatively clean biofuel.

Of all the technologies aimed at reducing emissions from the oil sands, carbon capture has attracted the most attention and the lion's share of government dollars to date. The biggest risk from carbon capture and storage, in my opinion, is that it might crowd out other interesting technologies aimed at reducing the footprint of the oil sands. The oil and gas industry spends only 0.9 percent of its budget on R&D, as opposed to 2 percent for industry in general. So the pace of, and investment in, innovation has not kept up with the challenges, particularly the environmental challenges.

But due to the mounting pressure coming from the public — and, increasingly, policymakers — big oil companies are starting to factor sustainability into production, something that can only come from new technology development. In fact, it's no small irony that the oil sands — undoubtedly the dirtiest project in Canada's history — could become a better testing ground for sustainable technologies than any other project in the country, and perhaps the world.

THE OPPORTUNITY TO DEVELOP sustainable technologies for the oil sands is drawing in some major players, including people like Ron Nolan. Nolan was the long-time CEO of Mississauga, Ontario–based Hatch Engineering, one of the world's largest engineering firms. But his main focus now is on a company called N-Solv Corporation. N-Solv claims it can reduce greenhouse gas emissions from some oil sands operations by as much as 85 percent. The company focuses on the bitumen deposits that sit too far beneath the surface for open mining. As noted above, these projects use steam-assisted gravity drainage to loosen the bitumen layer, thus allowing it to be pumped to the surface. This process requires massive amounts of natural gas to generate the steam, as well as large quantities of water. The N-Solv process relies instead on propane. Because propane needs to be heated only to 40°C, it reduces significantly the amount of energy required to extract bitumen, and eliminates completely the need for water.

I met with Nolan at the head office of Hatch Engineering in Mississauga. Nolan exhibits a low-key demeanour that perhaps stems from his simple roots growing up on an Alberta farm. Today, he still owns a working cattle ranch (on the day I meet with him, he tells me he has to leave early to drive some cattle to the United States). But if his style is modest and down-to-earth, his business career has been anything but low-key.

During his tenure with Hatch, Nolan oversaw a worldwide expansion during which the company's revenues grew tenfold. Today Hatch employs more than 4,500 people, and has a strong presence in markets all around the world. Although much of Hatch's focus is on the mining industry, Nolan imagines a return to the Alberta energy industry, where he first started his career (his first job was at TransAlta Power). This interest has led him to endow a chair in Sustainable Energy and Mineral Process Technologies at the University of Alberta.

Ron Nolan has seen the N-Solv technology through many stages, over many years. The original technology was developed by Dr. Emil Nenniger, who was a Hatch engineer when Nolan was CEO. Now, with Nolan as the chairman of N-Solv and Dr. Nenniger's son John as president, the company has demonstrated the technology through experiments at the Alberta Research Council. The results were so encouraging that the company managed to secure a partnership with Enbridge Ventures, a division of the natural gas company, and capital investment from Sustainable Development Technology Canada for a 500-barrel-a-day pilot plant. If they can prove the technology works at that pre-commercial scale, they can begin to deploy it in large-scale projects in the oil sands.

The potential is enormous. Not only could N-Solv's technology reduce the footprint of the large in situ operations (which account for an estimated 90 percent of all the bitumen in the oil sands), but it could do it cost-effectively. In fact, Nolan estimates that the N-Solv technology is much more profitable than the SAGD technology currently in use. If that's the case, it may not only radically increase the efficiency of in situ projects, but also increase the amount of oil sands bitumen that could be extracted for commercial use.

IT'S NOT JUST THE PROBLEM OF greenhouse gas emissions in the oil sands, however, that is attracting criticism —

water use is an equally important issue. Indeed, the
sheer volume of water used in the project is alarming: an estimated six hundred Olympic-size swimming
pools of new tailing ponds are added a day. But the
impact on wildlife is also large-scale. The 1,600 ducks
that died in a Syncrude tailings pond in 2008 elicited
national and international condemnation, and was
likely a tipping point for the industry to seek ways to
reduce its use of water.

A University of California chemical engineer named
David Soane is advancing a technology that would
separate the clay and sand in the tailings from the
water. The solids could then be put back into the open
mines, and the water could be reused in the processing
facility.

Soane is already a seasoned entrepreneur with an
impressive track record. His last company, Aclara Bio-
Sciences, was backed by Silicon Valley venture capitalists and acquired for $180 million. His new company,
Soane Energy LLC, based out of Cambridge, Massachu-
setts, has an impressive list of investors, including the
American multinational energy corporation Chevron.
If Soane can succeed at reducing the use of water in the
oil sands, there's little doubt that he will become even
richer.

THE OIL SANDS ARE MUCH MORE than a vast fossil fuel resource; they represent a unique opportunity to develop new technologies that can be exported globally, and applied to other "dirty" projects such as Venezuela's heavy oil deposits or even China's vast coal deposits. Canada can become a leader in more environmentally responsible fossil fuel production, which in a carbon-constrained world is likely to be a significant opportunity.

Of course, the principal demand for synthetic crude is for transportation, which is responsible for more than 30 percent of all emissions in Canada — more than power generation, the next largest contributor. Despite the move toward hybrids and electric cars, the majority of drivers still rely heavily on fossil fuels. That may change.

Already ethanol has been added to gasoline throughout Canada and much of the United States. But early support for ethanol fuels has wilted, as it has become clear that ethanol produced from most food sources — such as corn, for example — has limited, or even negative, impact on greenhouse gases. These findings have not stopped governments from advancing short-sighted legislation promoting the use of ethanol mixes in gasoline. But a consensus is slowly emerging that using food for the production of fuel generates limited energy efficiency and reductions in greenhouse gas emissions, while increasing the cost of food.

A much more promising potential lies in converting waste biomass into fuel ethanol. The resulting "cellulosic ethanol" could lead to dramatic reductions in greenhouse gas emissions from our transport fuel. It could also reduce our reliance on foreign oil and provide a potential new revenue stream for Canadian forest companies and farmers, who have by-products that were previously thought to have no value.

The potential market for cellulosic ethanol is huge. The 2007 U.S. Energy Bill calls for 21 billion gallons of cellulosic ethanol by 2022, and has spurred the development of the market with a tax credit of $1.01 per gallon. Other countries are also starting to heavily favour cellulosic ethanol over ethanol derived from food. A number of Canadian companies are leading the development of cellulosic ethanol, and stand to benefit from this massive market potential.

Perhaps the company that has progressed furthest in commercializing a cellulosic ethanol technology is Ottawa's Iogen Corporation, which is developing the use of enzymes to convert the cellulose in the feedstock into glucose that can in turn be processed into ethanol. With major investors such as Shell, Goldman Sachs, and Petro-Canada, Iogen was one of the first companies to test its process in a pilot plant. The company is now working on its first commercial plant in Prince Albert,

Saskatchewan, and is projected to process 750 tonnes
of waste cereal straw a day. But there are challenges. In
particular, the inability to process lignin — a chemical
compound that is part of the cell wall of most plants —
decreases the efficiency of Iogen's technology.

Other companies are using a thermochemical process to create a synthetic gas that can then be turned
into fuel ethanol, most commonly through the Fischer–
Tropsch process, which converts synthetic gas into hydrocarbons. The process was named after the German
scientists Franz Fischer and Hans Tropsch, who invented
it in the 1920s. Mississauga–based Woodland Biofuels is
taking the thermochemical process one step further by
putting the synthetic gas through a series of chemical
reactions to create a pure stream of ethanol. Woodland's
process can be used on any waste biomass, but the company concentrates primarily on wood waste, of which
Canada has plenty.

Greg Nuttall, has a compelling vision for the future,
one in which Canada becomes a biomass superpower.
Nuttall has been developing Woodland's process since
2005, when he became the company's CEO. He has a
background in law — practising in England for a time
and at the august Tory Tory DesLauriers & Binnington
in Toronto — but later he became a partner in an investment firm and a board member of Woodland before he

was asked to become CEO in 2005. Nuttall has built an outstanding team of engineers and managers, and has positioned his company to be a leader in the development of cellulosic ethanol.

With a large grant from the federal government through Sustainable Development Technology Canada and another from the Ontario government's Innovation Demonstration Fund, Woodland plans to build its first pilot plant in 2010, and, assuming it is successful, a full commercial plant shortly after. Using a process called Catalyzed Pressure Reduction™ (CPR™) technology, the company believes it can create fuel ethanol with limited negative by-products and greenhouse gas reductions at substantially less cost than any other technology. If in fact the system is inherently more efficient, it will help accelerate the commercialization of the technology.

A major limitation of bioenergy companies — including cellulosic ethanol producers — will be access to sufficient feedstock. A more efficient process requires smaller industrial plants, less feedstock, and more options for citing facilities. As demand for feedstock increases, these factors will become critical in determining whether companies like Woodland and its competitors can be commercially viable.

IF ENTREPRENEURS LIKE GREG NUTTALL are right, then in the future there will be no need to make fuel from food crops. And while that is probably a good thing for greenhouse gas emissions and for food consumers, it may be a mixed blessing for farmers, for whom ethanol provides a potentially lucrative market for their crops. As we will see in the next chapter, farmers are the custodians of perhaps our most undervalued resource, and they need all the help they can get.

Chapter Six

PEAK SOIL

IN EARLY SEPTEMBER OF 2009, my son and I drove up to Singhampton, Ontario, to visit the New Farm. The trip from Toronto is only two hours, but if you are paying attention the changing landscape also offers a lesson in the threats to one of our country's most valuable resources.

Just north of the city, you can't miss the countless new housing developments in various stages of completion. You may notice the rich brown earth where bulldozers have cleared the land, a fading vestige of the farmers' fields that used to thrive here. Every so often a farm remains, the barn and fields a lonely anachronism, a holdout against the inexorable spread of concrete. But you know it will not last long. For this is the land of the developers, and the site of one of the country's greatest building booms.

For anyone living in Toronto today, this development has been going on for so long that it has become a part of the regular unfolding of things. But when seen over the course of decades, the changes are astonishing. When I was young, my grandparents had a farm just north of the city, in the heart of an active agricultural community. As a boy I remember driving along quiet roads lined by barns and fields. Today, the farm is gone and has instead been replaced by row upon row of subdivisions.

Thirty minutes north of Toronto you will pass the sign for the Greenbelt, an initiative of the provincial government to preserve a ring of farmland and halt the unyielding spread of the city northward. Along with the much-heralded Places to Grow legislation, which aims to manage urban sprawl, the Greenbelt is the centrepiece of the government's efforts to halt the urbanization of Ontario's farmland and to force population growth into higher density areas.

Next, you will dip down into the Holland Marsh, a drained wetland of peat moss, where rich black earth stretches for kilometres and a variety of vegetable crops are now farmed. Eventually you will come to Barrie, once a fast-growing bedroom community and now a booming city in its own right. From there, if you turn northwest and drive another half hour, you will eventually reach the southern edge of Georgian Bay, where it turns from rocky archipelago to long sandy beaches. Trace the southern edge of the Bay going west, near to where the Niagara Escarpment abuts the edge of the water, and then turn south along the side of the escarpment. Soon you will arrive at the New Farm.

New Farm was launched by Brent Preston and Gillian Flies. In a time of increased urbanization, their story represents an interesting and hopeful counter-trend. Brent and Gillian met in Africa, where they were working as human rights activists for the Jimmy Carter Foundation. Throughout the 1990s they bounced around Africa, travelling to Malawi, Nigeria, and Liberia, before landing in East Timor in 1999. Caught up in the violence that swept the country during the election — their house was even bombed — they decided to return to Toronto and took day jobs in the city. Brent worked as a senior producer on the CBC show *CounterSpin*, and Gillian set up a successful consulting firm. They moved into the yuppie neighbourhood of the Annex, had children, and settled down to a comfortable existence.

A few years later, following a stint in Botswana, the couple decided they wanted to escape the city and try something different. They bought a farm in Creemore, Ontario, and started to think about a rural life. Gillian kept her consulting work in the city going, and Brent continued to write, but their passion for activism led them to consider other forms of community involvement. "We wanted to be part of the solution," Gillian says, "to make things better for our kids and other kids."

They weren't certain how to do that at first, but they felt it might involve building the community for local foods. On the side, they had developed a garden growing organic vegetables, which they would sell at the local farmers' market. Eventually they found themselves being approached by restaurants who wanted to buy their produce. They realized there was a growing demand for local, organic food that was not being met by most producers. So they expanded their garden and turned it into a full-scale farm, and Brent quit his job to work as a farmer full time.

Although Gillian had grown up on an organic farm in Vermont, this is Brent's first foray into farming, and I am keen to see how it's going. When we arrive, Brent is out in the fields with his kids, pulling up potatoes for lunch. My son dives right in, joining the other kids in the fields, up to his arms in earth and loving it. While the kids are busy harvesting vegetables for our lunch, Brent takes me on a tour. The first thing I notice is the incredible variety of crops.

"We grow just about everything," he says.

And he's not exaggerating. There are tomatoes, potatoes, cherries, beets, lettuce, carrots, peppers, and a good deal more.

Although the setting is idyllic, it's clear it's not easy work. While we walk along the edge of the fields, Brent explains that he has been working eleven hours a day, seven days a week, since May.

"I'm burnt out," he admits. This is his first day off in more than three months.

The day starts before sunrise, when Brent, Gillian, and four interns congregate on the porch with a pot of coffee before they start a long, gruelling day. Every hour counts, especially in the summer when the farm is most productive. They will earn much of their yearly income in twelve crucial weeks. On Sundays Brent drives to the nearby Creemore farmers' market, where he sells his goods to affluent consumers eager to purchase high-quality local produce. He also has a good business selling to high-end restaurants in Toronto that will pay a premium for their fruits and vegetables.

The good news for the New Farm — and one of the reasons Brent and Gillian decided to get into this business — is that there's a growing market for locally grown, organic food. They have a totally different business strategy than most farms, and one they admit that some of their neighbours find more than slightly odd. But those same neighbours perk up when they see that Brent and Gillian can sell lettuce for $8 a pound, which is more per pound than cattle ranchers get for beef. It's an appealing business model, at a time when most farmers are just scraping by, usually with the help of some off-farm income. So some of their neighbours have started to ask more questions about this whole organic thing.

Although the type of organic farming favoured by the New Farm has growing market potential, there's no doubt it's tough work and the hours of calorie-burning manual labour shows on Brent's tall, lean frame. The best varieties of vegetables are not given to mechanical methods — they are generally more brittle or fragile — and must be harvested by hand, which makes the work slower and harder. But it also makes the produce tastier, and more nutritious.

Part of this inherent value can be attributed to the soil. Many of Brent's neighbours tend to specialize in a specific crop and grow for volume. All too often for these farmers, soil nutrition and health is an afterthought, and they rely instead on chemical fertilizers to maintain their yields. This is not an option for Brent and Gillian who cut no corners when it comes to preserving the integrity of their soil.

While conventional farms regularly till the soil

("tilling and killing," as Gillian refers to it), turning over the plant roots and leaving soil exposed to the elements and therefore to erosion, at the New Farm they try to keep tillage to an absolute minimum. Brent and Gillian also plant nitrogen-fixing cover crops such as clover after any harvest. And they leave fields fallow for one year after every year of production. These methods preserve the quality of the soil.

Healthier soil, of course, leads to better farming conditions. An example of this benefit is soil compaction, which is a major problem for all farms. I had always imagined that compaction resulted mainly from farm equipment pressing down on the soil, thus causing it to lose pore space and its ability to absorb rainfall. This is one major cause, and a reason why at New Farm they are careful to leave walking lanes between plant rows. But Brent explains that compaction is also related to the health of the soil. The more living activity in the soil, the less it compacts. So healthier soil not only has the benefit of retaining water, it also has higher organic content, which provides nutrients for the plants.

It turns out that the earth is a lot more than rocks and dirt. In fact, it's a hive of microbial activity. Up to 1 billion bacteria — from as many as 15,000 different species — can live in one teaspoon of compost-rich soil. The job of the organic farmer is to harness and protect the fertility of the soil. Instead of being the master, the organic farmer is locked into a complicated and sometimes frustrating give-and-take relationship with the earth. When Brent sees that a part of his property is not growing well, he knows that he could throw a handful of nitrogen on it and that might take care of the problem. But for the organic farmer, that's verboten. And so he must look for other ways around the problem, in the interest of preserving a rigorous system that will maintain or even improve the health of the land.

When Brent finishes the tour, we head back to the house to set the harvest table and sit down to a late summer meal of barbecued hamburgers, potato salad, tomatoes, and lettuce. Our fresh bread comes from Michael Stadtlander, a local farmer and one of the world's most celebrated chefs. Stadtlander is famous for creating extraordinary meals made up only of local fare and served in his living room. City people — including myself on two lucky occasions — pay a pretty penny to experience this unconventional form of fine dining. Stadtlander built a bakery in nearby Singhampton, and he trades with New Farm, beans for bread. I ask how the arrangement works, and Brent says simply: "We give them a lot of beans, and they give us a lot of bread."

Although Brent and Gillian's decision to start a new career in organic farming was in part a decision based on their personal values, it also represents the potential for renewing one of the country's oldest industries, and with it new hope for preserving one of our most under-valued resources.

LIKE MUCH OF OUR INHERITED natural capital, our soil once seemed virtually infinite, but now it is looking more scarce and vulnerable than ever before. What many people don't realize is that this precious resource is ground zero in the fight against climate change. Soil is a source of potential sequestration of greenhouse gases through its organic content. But healthy soils can also mitigate the effects of climate change by holding and maintaining their mois-ture content, which may become critically important if increasing temperatures and droughts give rise to water scarcity. When we talk of critical natural resources, we sometimes forget the most obvious one — the one that's right under our feet.

Like many other potentially renewable natural resources, soil takes a great deal of time to create, but can erode quickly. Nature will take as much as five hun-dred years to create one inch of topsoil; aggressive farm-ing will deplete those nutrients in twenty-eight years. Over the last fifty years, the rate of soil depletion has increased worldwide, in part because of modern farming practices. As David Montgomery, professor of Earth and Space Sciences at the University of Washington, states in his startling book *Dirt: The Erosion of Civilizations*, "How we address the twin problems of soil degradation and accelerated erosion will eventually determine the fate of modern civilization."

The relationship between modern agriculture and soil depletion is complicated, but central to the story is the history of synthetic or inorganic fertilizers, one of the most transformative discoveries of the twentieth century. Before then, the world relied on organic fertilizers, primarily from animal manure. The discovery of deposits of seabird droppings — referred to as "guano" — on islands off the South American coast in the Pacific Ocean provided a potent natural source of nitrogen fertilizer for agricultural production worldwide. It also became a chemical source for explosives used in arms production. So valuable was the resource that the U.S. government passed the Guano Islands Act in 1856, which gave any American citizen the right to possess unclaimed land that contained guano deposits on behalf of the U.S. government.

Before the First World War, two German scientists named Fritz Haber and Carl Bosch developed a process to create synthetic fertilizer. The process was able to "fix" nitrogen from the atmosphere to produce ammonia.

The result was a synthetic nitrogen that replaced the need for guano in agricultural and arms production. When the First World War erupted, a naval blockade threatened Germany's access to guano deposits from Chile, and the German government turned to the process invented by Haber and Bosch for production of fertilizer and explosives.

The Haber–Bosch process, as it would come to be known, earned both men a Nobel Prize. More importantly, it led to a dramatic increase in food production throughout the twentieth century that resulted in unprecedented world population growth. Indeed, in the second half of the twentieth century alone, world food production doubled due to a sevenfold increase in the use of synthetic fertilizer. The Green Revolution in agriculture, spearheaded by American agronomist Norman Borlaug, championed industrialized agricultural practices, such as the use of synthetic nitrogen, to dramatically increase food production in developing countries. In the end, Borlaug's Green Revolution saved millions from starvation and earned Borlaug a Nobel Peace Prize.

In the process, however, an age-old connection between the soil and our food was severed. Prior to the development of synthetic fertilizer, our food production was connected fundamentally to the health of our soils. But afterward, soil fertility became slowly undervalued, and was seen merely as a medium through which synthetic nitrogen acted to fertilize food crops.

It has since become clear that agricultural productivity over long periods of time is still intrinsically tied to the fertility and health of the earth. Overreliance on synthetic fertilizer has been proven to gradually deplete the health of the soil, which means more synthetic fertilizers are required to maintain yields, thus further depleting soil quality; it's a vicious circle that has led to a slow decline in soil fertility in many parts of the world.

There are other problems associated with our reliance on synthetic fertilizers for food production. For one, the production of synthetic fertilizer uses vast amounts of energy and is heavily reliant on fossil fuels, a non-renewable resource. If the price of fossil fuels rises, this will in turn lead to increases in the cost of synthetic fertilizer, which could then put pressure on food production worldwide. In addition, nitrogen runoff from farmers' fields creates massive algae blooms in the oceans, killing huge swaths of sea life in a process called eutrification.

But the slow erosion of soil quality is the most troubling implication of our overreliance on modern agricultural systems. Age-old methods intended to maintain the natural fertility of the soils, such as crop rotation and use of nitrogen-fixing plants, have fallen increasingly out of favour. Instead, monoculture crops and a reliance on synthetic fertilizers has become the norm, and as a result the land is worked harder to generate larger yields. In addition, the growing use of pesticides can affect the microbial content in the soils. So while the industrialization of agriculture has brought with it many benefits, including increases in food production worldwide, it has also brought some unexpected consequences, including a slow decline in soil quality.

The intention of the early practitioners of organic farming was to return to heritage principles of food production. Whether organic produce is safer, on account of reduced pesticides, or more nutritious is still up for debate. Typically, in media discussions about organic farming, these potential health benefits are considered the primary rationale for buying organic. But a more provable benefit — one that is often forgotten in the discussion — is the effect on soil quality. On that count, the evidence in favour of organic farming is much stronger.

Numerous studies have now been undertaken to compare organic farming techniques with conventional farming techniques, and the results of those studies show that industrial farming using significant chemical fertilizers and pesticides can erode the fertility of soils over time. Organic farming, by contrast, can lead to a material gain in soil quality.

For example, a twenty-one-year-long study by the Research Institute of Organic Agriculture (FiBL) in Switzerland compared organic farming with two conventional systems. The study found that the organic system was superior to industrial farming in humus formation, soil calcium, soil pH, microbial biomass, and biomass from earthworms (what's called faunal biomass).

Similar results were drawn from a twenty-three-year-long study (the longest continuous study to compare organic and conventional farming practices) by the Rodale Institute, a Pennsylvania–based not-for-profit organization that promotes the benefits of organic farming. The Rodale study concluded that "while the portions of the field under conventional management have suffered further degradation from wind and water erosion, the portions under organic management have shown steady improvements in organic matter, water infiltration, microbial activity, and other soil quality indicators." Studies like these provide strong evidence of clear, tangible benefits to organic farming, chiefly its ability to preserve soil.

Although the best case for organic farming rests on soil preservation and health, it is not the only system to make these kinds of claims. Biodynamic farming, an agricultural system that predates the term *organic* and is characterized by treating the farm as a single biological organism, has also been shown to dramatically improve soil quality. A study of sixteen conventional and biodynamic farms in New Zealand by J. P. Reganold, a professor in the Department of Crop and Soil Sciences at Washington State University, found that "biodynamic farms proved to have soil of higher biological and physical quality than did the conventional farms," thus adding further evidence that alternative farming practices can have distinct advantages.

Organic and biodynamic farming are just two practices aimed at preserving organic content in soil and improving soil quality and fertility. Another prevalent practice is no-till agriculture, a process in which crops are grown without turning the soil. In addition to increasing organic matter and moisture content, and reducing soil erosion and runoff, no-till farming has the added benefit of reducing costs for farms, principally by saving on labour and fuel. Thirty percent of Canada's farmland is now no-till, and these farms are saving an estimated 3,051 terajoules of energy every year.

Because no-till agriculture increases the organic matter in soil and reduces the use of energy, it is a form of carbon sequestration that can potentially help to reduce greenhouse gas emissions in the atmosphere. As David Montgomery says in *Dirt*: "If every farmer in the United States were to adopt no-till practices and plant cover crops, American agriculture could squirrel away as much as 300 million tons of carbon in the soil each year, turning farms into net carbon sinks, rather than sources of greenhouse gases."

Sequestering carbon on farms will open them up to an important new revenue source: carbon credits. In Alberta, the first province with a viable carbon market in Canada, about half of all the carbon offset projects so far have been from no-till agriculture. By creating a financial incentive to adopt no-till practices, carbon markets may help to mitigate the trend toward soil loss.

But if soil loss from aggressive industrial agricultural practices is problematic, it's dwarfed by other causes, particularly by the kind of urbanization described at the beginning of this chapter. Although Canada is a vast country, in fact only 5 percent of the land mass is suitable for crop production. But this small sliver of land is being gobbled up at startling rates by urban Canada, which grew 80 percent — from 16 million to 24 million people — between 1971 and 2001.

Much of the growth in urban populations came at the expense of farmland. In fact, today cities and towns occupy 7.5 percent of the highest grade of agricultural land in the country — and a stunning 11 percent in Ontario, Canada's most fertile province. As a result, farmers have been pushed onto more marginal farmland, which exacerbates the problem of soil loss, since poorer soils require more intensive agricultural techniques to achieve reasonable yields.

This crisis is in part due to the collapse in farm incomes. As farming economies deteriorate, agriculture cannot compete against urban development in terms of land values. And as farmers continue to lose some of their best soil to urban sprawl, their incomes experience a further decline. It's a downward spiral. Today, it is estimated that half of all Canadian farmers support themselves through off-farm income. Brent Preston at New Farm believes that this is true of almost all of his neighbours. And though his wife is still employed part time as a consultant, they are working toward a day when their entire income is from farming. But if they do reach this goal, they will be the exception, not the rule.

The statistics paint a depressing picture. Gross income from Canadian farms decreased from a profit of $3.5 billion in 1986 to an estimated loss of $6 million in 2006. During that time, revenues grew from $21.4 billion to $36.1 billion. But costs grew even faster, from $17.8 billion to $36.1 billion. It's no wonder, then, that the total farm population declined from 3,289,140 to 727,125 between 1931 and 2001. With declining incomes and farm populations, and increased competition for the best land, the future for Canada's farms appears bleak.

So why are urban professionals like Brent Preston and Gillian Flies dropping their city jobs and running to the country to pick up a hoe?

WHILE AGRICULTURE IS FACING a real crisis in Canada, there are some countervailing trends that give cause for optimism, however faint. Urbanites are indeed eating up more of our agricultural land, but they are also eating up more local and organic foods, and showing a willingness to spend top dollar for it. In fact, organic farms grew in number from 2,230 to 3,444 in Canada between 2001 and 2006, a rare growth area in a depressed economy.

One of the great agricultural success stories in Canada has been the growth of Organic Meadow Inc., Canada's leading organic dairy company. Part of what makes Organic Meadow Inc. such a compelling story is that the company, probably the most visible organic brand in the country, is owned by the dairy producers themselves through their farmers' co-operative. It's a relatively unique arrangement. In most cases, little of the economic benefit for marketing, distributing, and selling food products accrue to the farmers. While the owners of food companies and brands have become richer, the farmer has been squeezed out. Organic Meadow, on the other hand, allows farmers to financially benefit from marketing and selling their own milk and dairy products.

One of my first introductions to the world of organic farming came from a trip to Ted Zettel's farm. Zettel is the current chairman of Organic Meadow Inc., but he was also a founder of the Organic Meadow Co-op. At the time, he was part of a very small group of organic farmers who were trying to get their products to market. They had a big vision. In his words, "the radical vision of the founders was of a separate model, a totally new food system that would deliver the highest quality, certified organic, local food to a willing, well-informed citizenry, who were more than happy to support the stewards of the land."

By the time I met him in 2003, Organic Meadow had grown into the country's largest organic brand. Its products graced the shelves of mainstream grocery stores such as Loblaws and Whole Foods. I drove to Zettel's farm near Walkerton — where he and his wife have raised six children — and sat down with him one afternoon. Zettel is a spry and fit man with an easy smile, a warm laugh, and a perpetual twinkle in his eye that puts people at ease and inspires trust. With brown hair and high cheekbones, he bears an uncanny resemblance to actor Willem Dafoe.

Sitting on the back porch of his farmhouse with a lemonade, I had an immediate appreciation of how important people like Ted Zettel are for a new industry. He saw very early on that organic agriculture was more than just a way of farming — it was about building a new industry, which required establishing a whole new infrastructure and supply chain. He had already been instrumental in founding the Ecological Farmers Association of Ontario (EFAO) in 1979, an organization whose goals included helping farmers to enhance the health of their soil.

But another objective of the EFAO was to create "links between farmers and consumers to gain their understanding, and to create markets for ecological farm products." Zettel's early involvement in the organic food movement was to apply useful entrepreneurial insight into an aging business model that in the end would serve the company — and the industry — well. First among these insights was to make a powerful and lasting connection between the farmer and the food buyer, which has been a critical aspect of the Organic Meadow mission and the principal explanation for the company's success.

If marketing insights are at the heart of the success of Organic Meadow, its origins were more about survival. The original co-op that has now evolved into Organic Meadow Inc. was formed in 1981, when the owner of the grain elevator with whom Ted and other organic farmers did business fell into financial difficulties. The owner

invited Ted and thirty other farmers to his house to discuss the situation. As Ted says now with tongue only
partly in cheek: "Had I known that the birthing and nurturing of what is now Organic Meadow, begun that fate-
ful evening, was to consume a good portion of my life, I
would have done the prudent thing and stayed home."

Fortunately he didn't stay home. Instead, Zettel
and the other farmers hatched a plan to form a co-op.
Each member had to put in $2,000 for working capital.
Together they made a deal to lease the property with
the creditors, and began to build a business. They kept
the name of the original grain elevator — OntarBio —
because they didn't want to spend the money to reprint
the marketing materials. Over time they would expand
their product base into dairy (now the largest part of
their business), and establish the new brand, Organic
Meadow. This expansion required lengthy and skill-
ful negotiations with the Dairy Farmers of Ontario, the
organization that controls milk supply in Ontario. But
today Organic Meadow represents more than fifty farms
spread across Ontario, and sells more than fifty different products, including milk, yogurt, ice cream, cheese,
grain, and eggs.

Organic Meadow's trump card has always been
the connection to the farmer. They have had to compete
head-to-head on many occasions with much larger food

companies, whose size and scale gave them economic advantages. But the consumer has continued to choose the authenticity of the Organic Meadow brand, preferring their products over others on the grocery store shelves.

Compared to other organic milk brands that cannot be tracked easily back to the dairy farmer, Organic Meadow proudly traces its path from field to fridge. And it turns out this connection is a powerful marketing tool. Knowing that the company is owned by the farmers — as opposed to a large food marketing company — is an important distinction for many shoppers. Not only do they feel the product is healthier and of higher quality, they tend to want to support farmers and their families. It makes for a competitive advantage that has served Organic Meadow well. The company is now expanding across the country; their products are available coast to coast, and they are developing producer groups in various provinces to provide local supply.

As Organic Meadow has grown, the producers in the Organic Meadow Co-operative have benefitted from its financial success. Not only are they paid what's called an MIP — a milk incentive premium on top of the normal price established by the milk marketing boards on account of producing organically — but as owners of the business they are eligible for dividends from the company. And while professional managers with food industry experience run the day-to-day operations of the company, farmers like Zettel still run the board and set the long-term strategy and direction.

The success of producer-owned food companies such as Organic Meadow is one example of an innovation in food marketing that is potentially changing the economics of agriculture, and opening up new opportunities for Canadian farmers. Perhaps more importantly, having financially viable producers who benefit from marketing their own products helps keep farmers in business, thus preserving the land and soil, and slowing the sprawl of urbanization.

ALTHOUGH MAINTAINING SOIL HEALTH IS critically important in terms of adapting to global climate change, there are other more technical approaches that don't address the issue of soil quality, but rather focus on developing plants that are better able to withstand climactic extremes. Although this approach is dramatically different from the one advocated by the New Farm or Organic Meadow, the two are not necessarily incompatible. In the end, the challenges we face are deep — and they may express themselves differently throughout the world.

Kingston, Ontario–based Performance Plants has more than one hundred patents and patent-pending applications that focus on developing crops that will be resistant to conditions associated with climate change — for example, maintaining yields in droughts or high temperatures. Working with the genes of specific plants that have the extraordinary ability to respond to extreme weather conditions — as opposed to using genes lifted from other species — Performance Plants looks to isolate those desirable traits and to amplify them. Or, alternatively, genes with undesirable attributes can be turned down. The result is plants with extraordinary abilities to respond to certain conditions, like a runner trained to excel in high altitudes.

Performance Plants was founded in 1996 by David Dennis, the former head of plant biology at Queen's University. His background in the food industry at Unilever helped him understand the advantages of building more resilient and hardy crops, especially in light of global climate change. Dennis explains the key to the Yield Protection Technology® (YPT®) that is the essence of the company's process: "We've made a molecular switch — the gene we've put in to modify the gene that's already in the plant turns on only when there's a drought. So when the plant is growing with plenty of water, it grows quite well as if we've done nothing to it at all. If the plant recognizes it's losing water, our system switches on to protect the plant. As soon as it gets more water, the gene switches off and the plant grows normally again."

Dr. Dennis developed the process first using the Arabidopsis plant, a weedy member of the mustard family that has a number of qualities that make it ideal for genetic manipulation. But Arabidopsis was only a test case. The company is now commercializing their process for more significant worldwide crops such as corn, rice, soybeans, and cotton. If the technology works on those crops, it could provide substantial advantages in feeding a growing world population in a time of climate change.

In 2009 Dr. Dennis passed the title of CEO to Peter Matthewman, a professional agrologist with an MBA and a long career in biotechnology and agriculture, including a stint overseeing the Life Sciences department at the Alberta Research Council. Under Matthewman's helm the company is steering a dual course. While continuing to develop the YPT technology for use in food crops, it is also aggressively working to develop modifications to bioenergy crops that would improve their characteristics for energy production. The company has partnered with Lafarge Cement, which wants to reduce its reliance on coal for cement kilns. Performance Plants hopes to eventually use the crops at the Lafarge plant in Bath, Ontario, which uses more than 100,000 metric tons of coal annually; the company hopes to reduce that quantity by 30 percent using bioenergy.

If companies like Performance Plants can improve the economics of growing bioenergy crops — such as switchgrass, miscanthus, or hemp — on marginal farmland, it could offer a double benefit of reducing greenhouse gas emissions and increasing the viability of farms. Perhaps it is not too surprising, however, that the future of agriculture is intertwined with energy production. This is only one of the interconnections between many of the industries I have spoken about in this book. While forestry, water, electricity, automobiles, fossil fuels, and agriculture have traditionally been regarded as distinct industries, the lines between these sectors are increasingly blurring and merging. These growing intersections form new areas of an emerging economy that is defined by a heightened understanding of the increasing scarcity of natural resources and the value of natural capital.

As OUR WORLD CHANGES RAPIDLY — driven in part by climate change and other environmental problems, in addition to demographic, economic, and geopolitical shifts — the resources that sustain us will come under additional pressure, and the industries that rely on these resources will encounter new challenges. But this process will also throw open new opportunities. Taking advantage of these opportunities will require a national strategy that lays the groundwork for a more innovative, green economy.

Epilogue

BUILDING A GREEN ECONOMY

I'M SITTING AT THE OMNI HOTEL IN Washington, D.C., for
Cleantech Forum XVIII, an international meeting place
for green investors and entrepreneurs. More than 500
attendees are packed into a large conference room to
hear the latest information about trends in environmen
tal investing, energy efficiency, and climate science, and
to listen to entrepreneurs with businesses running from
solar to geothermal to wind. The room is full of well-
heeled investors with billions of dollars to invest in the
next great green company.

First to take the stage is Michael Goguen, general
partner of Sequoia Capital, one of the world's leading

venture capital funds. Sequoia has invested more than $8 billion in technology companies, backing corporations such as Yahoo!, Google, and YouTube. Goguen's presence is evidence that clean tech has arrived as a mainstream sector of our economy. He talks about the opportunity that his firm sees in developing new clean-tech companies, which is why Sequoia has committed to step up their investments in this area.

Next up is Nick Parker, a Toronto–based entrepreneur and founder of the Cleantech Group. Parker is perhaps the world's pre-eminent flag bearer of the clean-tech future. He says that the clean-tech sector has seen more than $20 billion of venture capital investment since 2002, a 1,000 percent growth. Parker reminds the speakers that subsequent Cleantech forums will be held in India and Dubai in October, Israel in November, China in December, and Abu Dhabi in January. It's immediately clear that the investment in green technology has gone global, and that capital is moving quickly to solve some of the world's biggest crises and is making lots of money doing it.

But it wasn't always this way. I remember the first time I met Nick Parker in March 2001 in San Francisco, at the Energy and Environment Venture Forum, a predecessor organization to Cleantech. I had recently decided to start a venture capital business that focused on green technologies, and the Energy and Environment conference was the most established organization I could find to learn more about what was happening. Like the Cleantech group, it attracted investors and entrepreneurs who specialized in alternative power and other environmental technologies. But it was an underwhelming experience. Only about forty people, mostly angels and independent investors, had shown up. The mainstream captains of the investment industry were concentrating on the booming telecommunications sector and the Internet. Renewable energy was still considered a quaint idea or a quirky commercial niche, not a place to make serious money.

A lot has changed since then. Clean tech is now a growing investment field, drawing billions of dollars in capital and attracting some of the best minds in the world. Virtually all mainstream investment companies have an eye on this sector, from leading Silicon Valley venture capitalists, such as Sequoia, to large investment banks and pension funds. Gradually, over the last ten years, these investors have come to realize that great wealth awaits those who can solve our energy and climate problems. And this realization is driving the world's foremost venture capitalists to invest billions to find a clean-tech Google, and to make a fortune for themselves and their investors.

A study presented to the Rotman School of Business in 2007 by my colleague Greg Payne predicted that by 2030 an annual investment of $2.5 trillion was required to meet the basic environmental — and indeed the economic — challenges in areas such as water and energy infrastructure, and decrease the carbon content of our energy sources to forestall global climate change. The International Energy Agency has predicted a required investment of as much as $36 trillion by 2030 in low-carbon energy. Today the world spends roughly $300 billion a year in these areas, well short of even conservative estimates.

Mobilizing this capital will be critical to the success of all societies in the twenty-first century. Not only do our electricity, water, and transportation systems need maintenance and repair, but in the near future population growth, congestion, air pollution, resource constraints, and climate change will also have to be taken into account. These factors were not relevant in the early twentieth century, when the foundation of most of our modern infrastructure was first built.

Capital often moves in thematic waves, interspersed with recessionary periods when the excesses of the previous wave are digested and the seeds of the next are sown.[5] Sometimes capital gets it right and flows into

---

5 This theme was developed by my colleague, economist Greg Payne, from whom I am borrowing liberally here.

investments that provide social and economic benefits; sometimes it doesn't. The investment in technology in the 1990s — when we laid the fibre optic cable and built the Internet — led to a general improvement in productivity in society and left a number of important and lasting enterprises, such as Google or RIM. But the early years of this century were less successful. A fixation on unsustainable real estate and financial engineering led to the most serious economic collapse since the Great Depression, and did not leave much in the way of lasting value or extraordinary enterprises.

But there is a good chance that once we get through this recessionary period, capital will again get it right, and significant investment will flow into technologies and infrastructure that will make our economy more efficient and sustainable. With $500 billion in green stimulus announced by countries globally at the beginning of 2009, it appears that this next wave of capital investment is indeed gaining momentum and will go beyond investments in renewable energy. For, over time, the impact of the environmental and resource scarcity will be felt across our entire economy — just as the technology revolution at first had an impact on only a small part of the economy but over time transformed all sectors. Whereas we now think of "green jobs," we will eventually realize that the goal is the greening of all jobs. How we locate employees, the tools they use, the way they use energy and cars — all of these factors will be radically reframed to increase our efficiency and to reduce our footprint.

New environmental pressures are likely to increase over time, and our response to them now will factor heavily in our future economic success. We can play a defensive game, adapting and adjusting to the changes as they happen, or we can anticipate the changes to best take advantage of them. The second approach — the better one, in my view — will see the transformation of our economy as an opportunity to increase productivity and competitiveness. By being pre-emptive and anticipating the next evolution of our economy, Canada can achieve economic advantages by becoming a leader in resource efficiency and strengthening our natural capital. In doing so, we will also develop the technical expertise and know-how that we can sell around the world.

We must understand, though, that competition will be fierce, as many other countries are already moving aggressively to develop a green economy. China, for example, has invested hundreds of billions of dollars in renewable energy production, and is likely to triple its already aggressive projections by 2020. China now expects solar power production to grow to over 20,000 megawatts, a 75-fold increase in the next decade. Their solar manufacturers have driven down the costs of production by more than 30 percent, and China's solar industry, which includes global leaders such as Suntech Power Holdings and Yingli Green Energy, now commands one-third of the solar manufacturing market. In addition, China has announced plans to develop forty-two high-speed rail lines across the country, to establish a clean electricity grid, and to set clear targets for green energy production and for the reduction of carbon emissions.

So the question for Canada is: Will we be able to compete? So far, measured on the basis of green innovation and capital investment, Canada is falling behind. Sustainable Prosperity, a national policy and research network based at the University of Ottawa, has outlined a growing "low-carbon investment gap" in Canada compared to many other countries. They point out that Canada's 2009 stimulus package included roughly $3 billion for green stimulus, whereas the U.S. has earmarked more than $90 billion and China a staggering $221 billion. On a per capita basis, Canada has committed to only 0.2 percent of GDP in green stimulus. By comparison, the U.S. has committed 0.8 percent, Germany 1.2 percent, and China 2.73 percent. As a result of this investment gap, Canada is in danger of falling behind in building our critical infrastructure. Where other countries are already moving ahead on the next generation of high-speed rail, energy retrofits, and smart grid development, Canada is off to a slow start in an area that may well define our future economic competitiveness and prosperity.

There is arguably an even larger and more problematic low-carbon investment gap in Canada that has resulted from the collapse of investment in early-stage companies. According to the Canadian Venture Capital Association, only $25 million was invested in Canadian clean-tech companies in the second and third quarters of 2009. Global clean-tech investment was $1.59 billion in the third quarter of 2009 alone. These numbers are consistent with a general early-stage investment gap in Canada across all sectors. In fact, venture capital investment in Canada decreased by 35 percent between 2003 and 2008, from 0.13 percent to 0.085 percent of the GDP. Compare these figures to those in the United States, which has increased venture capital investment to 0.21 percent of GDP. In other words, Canada is investing less than half as much as our largest trading partner in new companies. So our current entrepreneurs are being held back at a time when the need for innovation has never been greater.

Equally troubling is an investment gap in technological innovation. With 1.9 percent of GDP invested in research and development, Canada is lagging well behind the average for the G7, which is around 2.2 percent, while a number of countries — including Israel, Sweden, Finland, Japan, and South Korea — are spending more than 3 percent of their annual GDP on R&D. Of course, many of these countries do not have the natural resources to fall back on that Canada does. In this respect, Canada's incredible resource base is also a curse, as it insulates us and prevents us from investing in the R&D that is required if we want to become a truly innovative economy. As a result Canada's biggest companies are still largely resource companies — predominantly mining and energy — and there are a scarce few Canadian companies that are true innovators on a world scale. Perhaps only RIM fits this description. So it appears that Canada is still captive to the forces that gave rise to Harold Innis's staples theory.

If Canada is to build a vibrant green economy, it will require closing these investment gaps. We need bold new policies to encourage R&D spending, especially in areas such as energy alternatives; policies to encourage venture capital investment, especially to start-up technology companies; greater technology transfer to move new ideas from universities and out into the marketplace; increased spending on green infrastructure in areas such as high-speed rail, public transit, and the smart grid; acceptance of higher energy costs, carbon taxes, cap-and-trade systems for large greenhouse gas emitters, and other kinds of ecological fiscal reform that puts a cost to pollution and a value to natural capital; and national standards for renewable energy production and energy efficiency. If we can begin to make these kinds of changes, Canada will be well positioned to participate in significant economic opportunity. But the country must take strong action and move aggressively in this new direction, or we will be left behind.

For Canada to truly compete in this next industrial revolution, the country will have to mobilize all of its potential and skills. We already have a patchwork of policies and areas of potential success to build on. Certain provinces are moving ahead in a variety of ways. For example, British Columbia has a carbon tax, the first in North America; Alberta has implemented a cap-and-trade program; and Ontario has established the far-reaching Green Energy Act, which includes a feed-in tariff for renewable energy.

At the federal level, too, there are some interesting programs. Sustainable Development Technology Canada has invested hundreds of millions of dollars in dozens of clean-tech Canadian companies (though ongoing funding is uncertain), and effective programs such as the Scientific Research and Experimental Development tax credits (SR&ED) support innovation and R&D spending. At the municipal level, as well, numerous activities are going on all across Canada. But the problem with these developments is that they are not coordinated in any meaningful way. So we are left with a patchwork of different programs and ideas announced by various levels of government with little coordination and overall planning.

To have a real hope of success and to compete with other countries that are moving aggressively to build a green economy, Canada needs to enact a national strategy that will leverage all of our strengths. Yet this is where we have failed most spectacularly. The unfortunate truth is that, today, Canada has virtually no national strategy on renewable energy; no plans for high-speed rail lines in development; no national smart-grid plans of any consequence; no greenhouse gas emissions reductions targets of any meaning; and no energy efficiency goals. In short, Canada is lacking a coherent national strategy on the most important economic questions of our time — questions that will define our future competitiveness, productivity, and prosperity.

This absence of a national strategy to develop the green economy is already costing us dearly. There is no way, of course, to measure the cost of the slow debasement of Canada's status and reputation in the eyes of the world, and even its own citizens, as a result of our abysmal record on greenhouse gas emissions, one of the very worst on the planet. But on a more practical note, we have compromised our ability to determine our own future, and forfeited our influence over how these systems will be designed.

Canada was in a position a number of years ago to make the transition to a low-carbon economy. But for the last fifteen years we talked ad infinitum, and did virtually nothing. So an opportunity was missed. There were numerous potential benefits to being an early mover. For one, we could have planned a more gradual transition, and given large greenhouse gas emitters time to learn how to monitor and manage emissions. As it turns out, our companies have no real experience in managing within any kind of carbon restraint at all. Had we initiated an effective cap-and-trade program years ago, it is much more likely that the TSX would now be the obvious exchange for carbon trading. More importantly, we might have designed the technologies and systems that could now be exported to other parts of the world. Canadian carbon sequestration technology would have been significantly advanced and perhaps ready to sell to the U.S. coal industry; the oil sands would be more energy efficient and less vulnerable to low-carbon fuel standards; and Canadian suppliers of low-carbon technology would be positioned to sell to the American market.

Each of these examples is a multi-billion-dollar missed opportunity. While taking early action would have caused our firms and industries to spend capital to adapt, the results would most certainly have been a dramatic surge in productivity, through increased investment in research and development in low-carbon technologies. As it stands, Canada's productivity has been declining, and we are less able today to take the dramatic steps that are required to retool our economy for the twenty-first century.

Until Canada is able to formulate a national strategy on climate change — as well as energy efficiency, transportation, the smart grid, and water infrastructure — we cannot expect to be a global player in the green economy. My point in writing this book, however, is to show that Canada still has the time and the potential to define a strategy for our companies and our economy to be leaders in green innovation. Our entrepreneurs are already pointing the way. Now we must follow their lead.

ONE OF THE DISTINGUISHING characteristics of entrepreneurs is their attitude toward risk. As an investor in early stage companies, I have been amazed at entrepreneurs' capacity to take risks that most others would not take. Throughout this book are examples of people who have mortgaged and leveraged their homes to invest all they have into their own companies, or accepted inadequate pay to provide the sweat equity to get their businesses off the ground. But the emotional risk — which is ultimately the risk of failure — is equally high. This is the fear of spending years investing in an idea that does not succeed, or the social humiliation of going out on a limb and failing. One of the most admirable qualities of entrepreneurs is their willingness to take on these kinds of risks to see their visions succeed. And the pressure that this induces causes them to be more focused on their goals.

Not all entrepreneurs succeed, of course, because the world is unpredictable and even the best may face unexpected challenges. People are never perfect, and entrepreneurs, like everyone, have flaws and blind spots that impair their ability to succeed. That's why some of the best entrepreneurs fail many times before they achieve their goals; the failures teach them lessons about themselves that are necessary for them to grow and acquire the self-knowledge to succeed. It's why entrepreneurship is so hard to teach — because the only real school is the school of real-world experience.

What accounts for the entrepreneur's capacity to embrace risk and accept the prospect of failure? I don't think they are more reckless than others; they are not daredevils who seek dangerous thrills. Rather, they measure and manage risk differently than others. A close analogy might be firefighters, who accept danger as part of what they do and who take precautions to minimize on-the-job hazards. The risks entrepreneurs take are carefully calculated, and the best entrepreneurs do everything in their power to understand the risks they are likely to face and to prepare for them.

The entrepreneur, then, is someone who accepts risk as an inevitable aspect of achieving a vision. It's the power and appeal of the vision that calls up the courage and stamina to face the prospect of failure. The visions of the entrepreneurs in this book are what drive them and provide the strength to accept and manage risk. Whether it's Chris Godsall's vision for providing green wood from flooded forests; Jim Lotimer's vision to measure our natural capital; Ian Clifford's vision of a battery that can power the world with renewable energy; Ron Nolan's vision of reducing the emissions of the oil sands; or Brent Preston and Gillian Flies's vision of building a viable model for organic farming: these people are willing to take risks in order to build a better future. I believe that these people are models for Canada, for our country must embrace risk and make sacrifices in the present in order to invest in our future.

But this will require a unique kind of leadership. The new entrepreneurs who are creating the sustainable companies of the future have cleared a path for others to follow. The vision is based on a new understanding of the value of our natural capital, and one that will hopefully compel our political leaders to establish a national strategy to build a green economy.

The way our current political game is played, parties compete to vilify and attack their opponents. But that game is also the principal cause of our country's current stagnation, as it prevents opportunities to develop broad coalitions for large national projects. We need politicians today who are willing to take the necessary risks to forge a new consensus around building a green economy in this country, the way the original political adversaries John A. Macdonald and George Brown did by joining together in the "Great Coalition" to create the British North America Act and to give rise to Confederation. In that case, the leaders realized that the political situation had descended into an unproductive standstill, and the only way to move forward was to work together to establish a new and better system. It took courage and the results today are unquestionable. So today we await new leaders who have the courage to take the political risks to forge a new "Great Coalition," and to develop a national strategy for a green economy and a new direction for the country.

So what will Canada look like in thirty years if we accept the challenge to develop a green economy? I suspect it will look much different than today. New technologies, new ways of producing low-carbon energy and using it more efficiently, and new forms of transportation will have been developed with an eye toward reducing our reliance on natural resources and diminishing our environmental footprint. If we do it well, we will be not only a less wasteful society, but a more prosperous society too.

The country will have moved beyond exporting raw materials to embrace the application of creativity, ingenuity, and technology in our economy. Alberta will have turned the oil sands from the most polluting project on the planet to the project with the largest application of sustainable technologies anywhere. Ontario will be a leader in manufacturing clean transportation options for road and rail. British Columbia will have leveraged its strength in the forestry industry to become a leader in the sustainable development of bioenergy. Nova Scotia will have developed a means to turn its tremendous tidal energy into sustainable power. Beyond all of these developments, though, the entire Canadian economy will have become dramatically more resource-efficient, using far less energy and water, and turning this efficiency into a sustainable competitive advantage.

These kinds of changes will require a higher investment in R&D across all sectors of our economy, a more successful technology sector, and a more innovative economy capable of building global companies and brands. It will be an efficient economy, where high standards of resource and energy efficiency create a competitive advantage for Canadian firms. The over-harvesting of natural resources will be replaced by a deeper understanding of the value of natural capital, and the value of preserving that natural capital for future generations.

In order to realize this vision, Canadians will have to adjust to a series of critical market reforms. In particular, environmental pricing will be accepted on the dual grounds of reducing environmental costs and building a more efficient economy. Programs such as carbon taxes, cap-and-trade programs, road pricing, and full costs for water usage would help to create a market for new technologies and a move toward greater efficiency. If the capital raised from these programs is diverted to reduce income taxes, the results will yield a more productive and robust economy, higher rates of employment, and a higher standard of living.

The country will also embrace a more overt entrepreneurial spirit. More of our capital will be invested in developing our own new businesses. Institutional investors such as large pension funds will again support early-stage companies, and, more broadly, there will be an attitudinal shift in favour of those who choose to start entrepreneurial endeavours. The typical antipathy toward risk-taking will be replaced by a more enterprising spirit, something similar to the robust attitude of the Nor'westers whose moxy — encapsulated in their motto "Fortitude in Distress" — helped to establish many of the vital institutions of our country. In this we will also take a page from our enterprising neighbours to the south, whose entrepreneurial culture encourages people to take risks to start new businesses. So we, too, will establish the conditions to help entrepreneurs succeed. And as a culture we will learn to both admire them when they succeed, and respect them when they fail.

Yet in many respects, all of these changes are already taking place, on account of the actions of thousands of people across Canada. These new entrepreneurs are designing the systems and tools, developing the technology, and marketing the products that are helping the world reduce its greenhouse gas emissions. They are providing clean drinking water through new water filtration technologies; delivering low-carbon energy that powers a smarter electricity grid and a smart car; reducing emissions from fossil fuel production, developing sustainable forestry technologies; and preserving the vital resources of the soil.

In short, they are providing the vision and leadership required to build a green economy for the future. And it is a future in which society will prosper.

I REMEMBER THE DAY WHEN I realized for myself that I was a Canadian — I mean the first time I really, authentically understood what that meant.

I was at the Ramada Inn in Thunder Bay. A funny place to have an epiphany, I know, but there I was in a corner room that had two large windows looking out on the stunningly beautiful Lake Superior. The shadow of the peninsula, Sleeping Giant, was still visible at dusk. It was my first day off during my second year of tree planting, and I had driven in from camp with some friends to hit the "big city," have a good time, and let off some steam. We'd been told that the Ramada had an unwritten policy to turn tree planters away, but we'd sent the cleanest of our group to the check-in and somehow gotten the keys. So there we were, all cleaned up, having a beer, and ready to hit the town. But the civilization of the hotel felt so good, we thought maybe before we went out we'd watch a little TV.

Knowlton Nash, then anchor of the CBC's national news program, was on the tube. We sat and watched the stories that were consuming the nation's attention. Fish stocks were low in Newfoundland, causing problems for the fishermen, the local communities, and the economy of the entire province; meanwhile, in the West, fires were chewing up large swaths of Alberta and British

Columbia, and stalwart firemen were shown emerging from the bush with charcoal faces.

For some reason we were enthralled by these stories, which on one hand played out like tragedies of Shakespearean proportions, and on the other hand were nothing more than the usual unfolding of the country's daily trials and tribulations. It felt like we were living out Marshall McLuhan's vision of a global village. In that hotel room, right in the geographical middle of this enormous country, with dirt on our hands even after a shower, I felt for the first time like a full member of that village.

My tree-planting companions and I sat and watched the news. No one talked. I suspect that most of them would remember that moment as I do: a seminal moment when an identity was briefly understood. The essence of my realization was how the natural resources of the country were interwoven with our economies and our communities, and were the foundational core of our identity. Perhaps the lesson stayed with me in part because of the work we were doing ourselves, planting trees out in the remote forests of Northern Ontario. But for whatever reason, it left me with a lasting impression about how this country was built from the earth, forests, fish, energy, minerals, water, and soil.

From the beginning, Canadians have lived close to the natural world. Even when our livelihood has been in some kind of conflict with nature, there has always been an appreciation, an understanding, a respect. The land was both a grounding force, providing a sense of identity, history, and connectedness; and also a nurturing force, providing our sustenance and wealth. But our relationship to the land is changing. As our populations move into cities, we lose that ancient connection to the environment. As we rely on others for our life and sustenance — be it food, water, or energy — we become disconnected from the world around us. Perhaps it is ironic, then, that our most intractable environmental challenge, the threat of climate change, may remind us again of our fundamental connection to the natural world.

So we are slowly arriving at an important new understanding. It is now possible to recognize that in the long march of human history, the last hundred years have been a short phase, an extraordinary time of unparalleled growth and prosperity. But this prosperity was by definition temporary. Natural boundaries and limits have asserted themselves, either through the depletion of cheap energy or through growing environmental problems.

And so now we are starting to understand that this was but one stage that will come to an end, and we must look for a new way forward. For Canada and Canadians, this realization provides a new opportunity to work together toward a common project that will require co-operation, capital, commitment, and the acceptance of risk. And that project is the building of a green economy.

NOTES

Introduction: A Land of Scarcity

For more on the North West Company, a.k.a. the "rampaging free enterprisers of the North American frontier," see Peter C. Newman, *Caesars of the Wilderness* (Markham, Ont.: Penguin Books, 1987). This, the second volume in a trilogy on the Hudson's Bay Company, is the classic text on the North West Company. Much of the detail on the fur trade, including the number of furs sold by the company, comes from this source. I have quoted specifically from pp. xvii and 7.

Harold A. Innis developed the "staples thesis" to explain how the Canadian economy had become reliant on natural resources. See his books *The Fur Trade in Canada* (Toronto: University of Toronto Press, 1970), and *Essays in Canadian Economic History*, edited by Mary Q. Innis (Toronto: University of Toronto Press, 1956).

Jared Diamond's book *Collapse: How Societies Choose to Fail or Succeed* (New York: Penguin, 2005) is a comprehensive and thoughtful analysis on what makes societies go extinct. Diamond's discussion of "rational bad behaviour," the institutionalized economic misalignments that lead to trouble, are discussed on p. 430.

The introduction to the concept of the Tragedy of Commons was made by Professor William Forster Lloyd in his pamphlet *Two Lectures on the Checks to Population* (Oxford: Printed for the author, 1833).

The term "Tragedy of the Commons" was first coined and popularized by Garrett Hardin in *Science*, Vol. 162 (13 December 1968), pp. 1243–8.

Specific information on Sweden's positive environmental experiment came from Mitch Potter, "The Low-Carbon Diet," *Toronto Star* (27 September 2008), accessible at <http://www.thestar.com/federalelection/article/507303>, and Stanley Reed and Ariana Sains, "Sweden Puts Its Bets on Green Tech," *Spiegel Online* (19 January 2009), <http://www.spiegel.de/international/business/0,1518,601997,00.html>.

The seminal report on the effectiveness of carbon taxes, energy taxes, and other examples of environmental fiscal reform was prepared for the European Commission by a project called COMETR (Competitiveness Effects of Environmental Tax Reforms). The report is called *Carbon-Energy Taxation: Lessons from Europe* (London: Oxford University Press, 2009). A copy of the summary report can be found at <http://www.dmu.dk/cometr/COMETR_Summary_Report.pdf>.

Facts about the German solar market were taken from the *New York Times* (16 May 2008). And facts on Japan's experience with energy efficiency came from the *Globe and Mail*, Report on Business (21 May 2008), and the *Washington Post Foreign Service* (16 February 2006), p. A01.

Japan's reduced consumption of oil is reported in Marcus Gee's article "As Oil Soars, Japan's Plan Makes Sense," *Globe and Mail* (21 May 2008).

Chapter One: If a Tree Falls

For more on the economics of the British Columbia forest products industry, see links to forest industry statistics on the Council of Forest Industries website at <http://www. cofi.org/library_and_resources/default.htm> (source: Natural Resources Canada website, <http://cfs.nrcan.gc.ca/index/forestindustryincanada>).

Many of the statistics related to the impact of the pine beetle on B.C. forests came from "Responding to the Challenge of the Mountain Pine Beetle," a discussion paper prepared by Don Wright for the Business Council of British Columbia and the Council of Forest Industries in December 2007, <http://www.bchc.com/Documents/EC 20071214_PineBeetlePaper.pdf>.

A source for worldwide demand for biofuels came from the United Nations Economic Commission for Europe (UNECE) press release, "UNECE/FAO Forest Products Annual Market Review, 2008–2009: Forest products markets badly hit by the crisis but use of wood energy on the rise" (Geneva, 4 August 2009), <http://www.unece.org/press/pr2009/09tim_po4e.htm>.

Information about the bioenergy potential from Ontario's forests can be found in the BIOCAP Canada Foundation report "Exploring the Potential for Biomass Power in Ontario," <http://www.biocap.ca/files/Ont_bioenergy_OPA_Feb23_Final.pdf>, p. 3.

An outstanding source on avoided deforestation, and in particular the economics of avoided deforestation, is Nicholas Stern, *The Global Deal: Climate Change and the Creation of a New Era of Progress and Prosperity* (New York: Public Affairs, 2009). See p. 148 in particular. I have also referenced Stern's original report to the British Parliament, *The Stern Review on the Economics of Climate Change*; see <http://www.hm-treasury.gov.uk/stern_review_report.htm>.

A further study on the economics of REDD which I used as a source was "Policies to Reduce Emissions from Deforestation and Degradation (REDD) in Tropical Forests: An Examination of the Issues Facing the Incorporation of REDD into Market-Based Climate Policies," by Erin C. Myers, <http://www.rff.org/documents/RFF-DP-07-50.pdf>.

For the value of the Canadian boreal forest, see "Counting Canada's Natural Capital: Assessing the Real Value of Canada's Boreal Ecosystems" (25 November 2005), a Pembina Institute study authored by Mark Anielski and Sara Wilson and prepared for the Canadian Boreal Initiative. I quoted specifically from p. 2.

Chapter Two: Water, Water Everywhere

The specific study cited by Natural Resources Canada's project, "Enhancing Resilience in a Changing Climate," which points to the possibility of the Great Lakes once again becoming "terminal," is by Thomas E. Croley II and C. F. Michael Lewis: "Warmer and Drier Climates that Make Terminal Great Lakes," *Journal of Great Lakes Research* 32 (2006), 852–69, <http://www.glerl.noaa.gov/pubs/fulltext/2006/20060043.pdf>.

I relied heavily on Chris Wood's book on water for many of the facts on our reliance on water. See *Dry Spring: The Coming Water Crisis of North America* (Vancouver: Raincoast Books, 2008). Information about reliance on water for manufacturing is on p. 18; about changes to shipping, on p. 123; and about water use in the oil sands, on p. 180. For decreases in water flow in Western Canada, see p. 166.

Statistics on changes in hydroelectric power and fish habitat with changing water levels were provided by Environment Canada's National Water Research Institute, which can be found on the Government of Canada's Depository Services Program website at <http://dsp psd.pwgsc.gc.ca/Collection/En1-28-1-2000-02E.pdf>.

Information on water withdrawal and uses came from Environment Canada, <http://www.ec.gc.ca/eau-water/default asp?lang=En&n=851B096C-1#agriculture>.

For the impact of water scarcity on Alberta, see "An Impending Water Crisis in Canada's Western Prairie Provinces," co-authored by W. F. Donahue and David Schindler of the University of Alberta (25 February 2006). The article was published in *Proceedings of the National Academy of Sciences of the United States of America* (PNAS), 103(19) (9 May 2006), pp. 7207–9.

Statistics on the changes in levels of Lake Mead and the flow to the Colorado River are cited in an article entitled "Lake Mead Could Be Dry by 2021" on the University of California website at <http://www.universityofcalifornia.edu/news/article/17297>.

Information about the Ogallala Aquifer is from BBC News, "World Water Crisis," <http://news.bbc.co.uk/hi/english/static/in_depth/world/2000/world_water_crisis/default.stm>.

Polling on Canadians' attitudes to water was quoted in Linda Diebel's article in the *Toronto Star*, "Guard Resources, Ottawa Urged" (15 April 2008), <http://www.thestar.com/article/414557>. This article also references Peter Lougheed's views on the U.S. grab for Canadian water resources.

The Montreal Economic Institute's proposal to sell water resources to the U.S. was reported in an article by John Partridge, "Quebec Think Tank Favours Water Exports," *Globe and Mail* (27August 2008).

Estimates of 50 million environmental refugees by 2050 came from a report from the Institute for Environment and Human Security of United Nations University (UNU–EHS). See "As Ranks of 'Environmental Refugees' Swell Worldwide, Calls Grow for Better Definition, Recognition, Support" (12 October 2005), <http://www.ehs.unu.edu/article:130>.

Effects of water scarcity on sub-Saharan Africa were reported in *Harper's* (September 2007), p. 47.

Details on water prices in different countries is available from the Conference Board of Canada, <http://www.conferenceboard.ca/HCP/Details/Environment/water-consumption.aspx#water>.

The OECD report on water consumption in different countries can be found online at <http://www.oecd.org/dataoecd/42/27/34416097.pdf>.

A report on the size of the water market, "Water Cultivation: The Path to Profit in Meeting Water Needs" (31 October 2008), was released by the Lux Research Water Intelligence service.

Information on sickness from water-borne diseases in developing countries can be found in a UNICEF/World Health Organization report, "Diarrhoea: Why Children Are Still Dying and What Can Be Done" (October 2009), <http://www.unicef.org/health/files/Final_Diarrhoea_Report_October_2009_final.pdf>.

Information on the desalination market was taken from "Desalination Markets 2005–2015: A Global Assessment and Forecast," 1st edition (April 2004), a report researched and compiled by Christopher Gasson and Peter Allison for Global Water Intelligence and accessible at <http://www.idswater.com/Common/exhib_6/Desalination%20Markets%20Contents.pdf>.

Much of the information on declines in fish stocks comes from Alanna Mitchell's *Sea Sick* (Toronto: McClelland & Stewart, 2009). Mitchell also cites (on p. 132) a *Science* article (Vol. 314, 3 November 2006, pp. 787–90) that predicts "the total collapse of all commercial fisheries by 2048 unless practices change."

Chapter Three: Electric Avenue

For further information on emissions from the power industry, see *North American Power Plant Emissions*, a report prepared for the Commission for Environmental Cooperation (CEC) of North America and authored by Paul J. Miller and Chris Van Atten. It is accessible at <http://www.cec.org/files/pdf/POLLUTANTS/PowerPlant_AirEmission_en.pdf>.

Information on the cost of building a new nuclear reactor was taken from the Investeco Capital Newsletter (November 2009), <http://investeco.com/uploads/file/investeco%20newsletter%20nov09.pdf>.

The quotation from Dr. John MacDonald, CEO of Day 4 Energy, was taken from the *Globe and Mail* (19 October 2009), p. B10.

The estimate of power resource available from low-head hydro power comes from CanmetENERGY, a clean energy research group working within Natural Resources Canada. For low-head hydro estimates, see <http://canmetenergy-canmetenergie. nrcan-rncan.gc.ca/eng/renewables/small_hydropower/low_ head_hydro.html>.

The development of the negawatt is taken from Amory Lovins's article "The Negawatt Revolution," *Across the Board*, 27(9) (September 1990). See also "The Negawatt Revolution: Solving the CO_2 Problem," Lovins's keynote address to the Canadian Coalition for Nuclear Responsibility (CCNR) Green Energy Conference in Montreal, 1989, at <http://www.ccnr. org/amory.html>.

The report on the jobs created by energy efficiency investment is from Deutsche Bank Advisors: "Economic Stimulus: The Case for 'Green' Infrastructure, Energy Security and 'Green' Jobs" (November 2008).

Chapter Four: Who Revived the Electric Car?

Information on the Canadian automotive industry is from the National Research Council Canada, <http://www.nrc-cnrc. gc.ca/eng/sectors/automotive.html>.

Information on the decline of the Canadian automotive industry during the recent downturn comes from the Conference Board of Canada, *Canada's Motor Vehicle Manufacturing Industry: Spring 2009*. See <http://www.conferenceboard.ca/documents.aspx?DID=3051> for more information on the report.

The source on Better Place is Daniel Roth's article, "Driven: Shai Agassi's Audacious Plan to Put Electric Cars on the Road," *Wired* (September 2008), <http://www.wired.com/cars/futuretransport/magazine/16-09/ff_agassi>.

Chapter Five: An Energy Superpower

For a good discussion of the concept of EROI, see Thomas Homer-Dixon, *The Upside of Down: Catastrophe, Creativity and the Renewal of Civilization* (Toronto: Alfred A. Knopf Canada, 2006).

Information on environmental groups dropping out of the Cumulative Environmental Management Association (CEMA), the group established by the Alberta government to review environmental practices in the oil sands, comes from a release by the Pembina Institute, "Environmental Groups Pull Out of Multi-stakeholder Oil Sands Process" (August 18, 2008). See <http://www.pembina.org/media-release/1678>.

Information about the use of natural gas in the oil sands comes primarily from a report by the National Energy Board entitled *Canada's Oil Sands: Opportunities and Challenges to 2015: An Update* (June 2006), accessible at <http://www.neb.gc.ca/clf-nsi/rnrgynfmtn/nrgyrprt/lsnd/pprtntsndchllngs20152006/pprtntsndchllngs20152006-eng.pdf>.

Information on growth in emissions from the oil sands comes from the OECD's report, *Economic Survey of Canada 2008* (11 June 2008).

On the scope of the opportunity for carbon capture and storage, see Annie Jia, "Researchers Examine Carbon Capture and Storage to Combat Global Warming," *Stanford Report*, Stanford University (13 June 2007), <http://news-service.stanford.edu/news/2007/june13/carbon-061307.html>.

The visit by South Carolina senator Lindsey Graham to the International Test Centre for CO_2 Capture in Regina was covered in *Maclean's* by Nicholas Kohler (22 September 2009); see <http://www2.macleans.ca/2009/09/22/in-conversation-with-sen-lindsey-graham/>.

Information on the likelihood that CO_2 will remain stored by CCS technology is from a Special Report of the International Panel on Climate Change (IPCC). See Bert Metz, Ogunlade Davidson, Heleen de Coninck, Manuela Loos, and Leo Meyer, eds., *Carbon Dioxide Capture and Storage* (Cambridge: Cambridge University Press, 2005).

Oil and gas sector investment in R&D is cited in the *Globe and Mail* (25 April 2009), p. B4.

The British trade office in Calgary estimates that it has introduced 150 companies to the area in 2009 alone, many of which are introducing new technology developed in the North Sea oil fields. See Nathan Vanderklippe, "Why the British are Invading the Oil Patch," *Globe and Mail* Report on Business (6 September 2009), <http://v1.theglobeandmail.com/servlet/story/RTGAM. 20090906.british07/BNStory/Business>.

Information on the percentage of emissions that come from transportation is sourced from Environment Canada's online web magazine, *EnviroZine*. See "Canada's Greenhouse Gas Emissions Are Down," *EnviroZine*, Issue 37 (13 November 2003), <http://www.ec.gc.ca/EnviroZine/english/issues/37/feature3_e.cfm>.

Chapter Six: Peak Soil

Much of my research and facts on soil erosion comes from the startling book *Dirt: The Erosion of Civilizations*, by David R. Montgomery (Berkeley: University of California Press, 2007). On carbon sequestration of no-till agriculture, see p. 213.

Information on the Rodale study on conventional versus organic farming can be found online at <http://newfarm.rodaleinstitute.org/depts/NFfield_trials/0903/FST.shtml>.

The study of biodynamic farming in New Zealand is entitled "Effects of Biodynamic and Conventional Farming on Soil Quality in New Zealand," by J. P. Reganold of the Department of Crop and Soil Sciences, Washington State University (1996). See <http://www.infrc.or.jp/english/KNF_Data_Base_Web/PDF%20KNF%20Conf%20Data/C3-3-071.pdf>.

Statistics on the percentage of farmland that is no-till comes from Attah K. Boame's article "Zero Tillage: A Greener Way for Canadian Farms," in *VISTA on the Agri-Food Industry and the Farm Community* (November 2005), <http://www.statcan.gc.ca/pub/21-004-x/21-004-x2005006-eng.pdf>. The *VISTA* newsletter is published by the Agriculture Division of Statistics Canada.

For statistics on the loss of farmland to urbanization, see "The Loss of Dependable Agricultural Land in Canada," by Nancy Hofmann, Giuseppe Filoso, and Mike Schofield, in Statistics Canada's *Rural and Small Town Canada Analysis Bulletin*, Vol. 6, No. 1 (January 2005), <http://www.statcan.gc.ca/pub/21-006-x/21-006-x2005001-eng.pdf>. See also Statistics Canada, *The Daily* (31 January 2005).

Statistics on farm income and the number of organic farms come from Statistics Canada's *Census of Agriculture* and *Agriculture Overview, Canada and the Provinces*.

Quotations from David Dennis on Yield Protection Technology® (YPT®) is from "Plant Performance," an article by Stephanie Fehr in *Germination: The Magazine of the Canadian Seed Industry* (January 2007), pp. 4–6. See <http://www.seedquest.com/hosting/germination/archive/articles/07/DavidDennis.pdf>.

Epilogue: Building a Green Economy

The International Energy Agency (IEA) predictions on investments in energy are from "New Energy Realities: WEO Calls for Global Energy Revolution Despite Economic Crisis" (12 November 2008), <http://www.iea.org/press/pressdetail.asp?PRESS_REL_ID=275>.

Developments in Chinese efforts to develop solar technologies were sourced from an article by Keith Bradsher, "China Racing Ahead of U.S. in the Drive to Go Solar," *New York Times* (24 August 2009), <http://www.nytimes.com/2009/08/25/business/energy-environment/25solar.html>.

Canada's "low-carbon investment gap" was discussed in a report entitled "The Low Carbon Investment Gap: A Discussion Paper," *Sustainable Prosperity* (November 2009).

Statistics on Canadian clean-tech venture capital investing were reported in "Global Cleantech Venture Investment Rebounds (but not in Canada)," Investeco Capital Newsletter (November 2009), <http://www.investeco.com/uploads/file/investeco%20 newsletter%20nov09.pdf>.

Information on investment in R&D in Canada comes from *State of the Nation 2008 – Canada's Science, Technology and Innovation System,* published by Canada's Science, Technology and Innovation Council. See <http://www.stic-csti.ca/eic/ site/stic-csti.nsf/eng/h_00011.html>.

BIBLIOGRAPHY

Diamond, Jared. *Collapse: How Societies Choose to Fail or Succeed.* New York: Penguin, 2005.

Friedman, Thomas L. *Hot, Flat, and Crowded: Why We Need a Green Revolution and How It Can Renew America.* New York: Farrar, Straus, and Giroux, 2008.

Gelbspan, Ross. *The Heat Is On: The High Stakes Battle over Earth's Threatened Climate.* Reading, Mass.: Addison-Wesley, 1997.

Hawken, Paul. *The Ecology of Commerce: A Declaration of Sustainability.* New York: HarperCollins, 1993.

Homer-Dixon, Thomas. *The Ingenuity Gap.* Toronto: Random House of Canada, 2001.

_____. *The Upside of Down: Catastrophe, Creativity and the Renewal of Civilization.* Toronto: Alfred A. Knopf Canada, 2006.

Innis, Harold A. *Essays in Canadian Economic History.* Ed. Mary Q. Innis. Toronto: University of Toronto Press, 1956.

_____. *The Fur Trade in Canada.* Toronto: University of Toronto Press, 1970.

Mitchell, Alanna. *Sea Sick: The Global Ocean in Crisis.* Toronto: McClelland & Stewart, 2009.

Monbiot, George. *Heat: How to Stop the Planet from Burning.* Toronto: Doubleday Canada, 2006.

Montgomery, David R. *Dirt: The Erosion of Civilizations.* California: University of California Press, 2007.

Newman, Peter. *Caesars of the Wilderness.* Toronto: Penguin Books, 1987.

Porter, Michael. *The Competitive Advantage of Nations.* New York: The Free Press, 1990.

Stern, Nicholas. *The Global Deal: Climate Change and the Creation of a New Era of Progress and Prosperity.* New York: Public Affairs, 2009.

Wood, Chris. *Dry Spring: The Coming Water Crisis of North America.* Vancouver: Raincoast Books, 2008.

ACKNOWLEDGEMENTS

There are many people who directly or indirectly helped in writing this book.

I'd like to thank friends Stephen Smith, Sarah Powell, Michael McGowan, Shelagh McNulty, Gerald Butts, Tammy Quinn, Martha Sharpe, George Butterfield, Martha Butterfield, Liz Rykert, Miles Kronby, John Sewell, Stewart Elgie, and John Ketchum. All of these friends have helped in important respects during the writing of this manuscript.

I'd like to thank Nick de Pencier, Jennifer Baichwal, and Greg Kiessling for their friendship, but also for reading the manuscript and providing feedback.

I'm grateful to all of the people at House of Anansi Press, but particularly my editor, Janie Yoon, whose editorial commentary was insightful and invaluable.

I would like to mention and recognize the CEOs and managers I work with, in particular those who are not noted elsewhere in this book, including Jamie Cooney, Ron Francisco, Terri Newell, Peter Bruijns, Thomas

Schneider, Berndt Schneider, Phil Whiting, Steve Cavell, and Rick VanSant.

I would like to mention Dalton McGuinty, whom I have had the privilege of advising on some of the issues that are discussed in the book. I also would like to recognize the hard-working people in his office, particularly Jamison Steeve, whom I have enjoyed working with over the last few years, and also all those who have participated in the Premier's Climate Change Advisory Panel, including Rachel Kampus of the Climate Change Secretariat.

I'd like to thank all of the people at 70 The Esplanade, including Laurie Simmonds and the whole Green Living team, Grant Gordon and the folks at Key Gordon, as well as Diane Dawson, Anne O'Connor, Kasia Hulicki, Alexandra Zawadzka, and Carole-Ann Hayes from Key Publishers.

I owe a debt of gratitude to all of my partners at Investeco Capital, including Michael de Pencier, with whom I founded the company many years ago and who has been a constant source of support and thoughtful advice. Also: John Cook, a close friend who is full of insight about the green economy and on what it takes to build great companies; Stephen Griggs, who has brought new and important perspectives to our work at Investeco; Chuck Holt, whose energy and talent has been invaluable; and Greg Payne, whose ideas on the green economy are as insightful and coherent as those of anyone I know. I feel privileged to work with all of you.

I want to make a special mention of two of my co-workers in particular, the two I have spent the most time with building our business, and whose ideas and personalities have greatly influenced me: Michael Curry and Alex Chamberlain. Over countless hours we have driven the highways and back lanes of Ontario looking for the next great, green company to back. In all that time, as we drove through the agricultural heartland of our province, or through the industrial parks where the economic pulse of our nation is ever beating, we talked about our companies, our friendships, our families, and above all our desires to live lives with meaning and purpose. Those conversations have had a powerful impact on me, and in large part made me want to write this book.

I owe a special debt to Evan Solomon, my business partner in my first venture, *Shift* magazine, who worked as a co-editor on two books of related topics, and who read a very early draft of the manuscript and pointed me in a good direction. Since I met him — a bright-eyed kid at McGill on St. Laurent Street in 1987 — we have never been far apart, and perhaps more than anyone I have been influenced by his enthusiasm for learning, and his fearlessness in moving forward into new adventures.

To Tom, my brother, I owe an equally great debt. He was the one who introduced me to the idea of a sustainable economy. He was the one who went looking for a way to combine his interests with his career, and provided me with ideas of how I could do the same. Ours has been a shared path, like two branches of the same tree.

I owe a debt of gratitude to my parents Tom and Mary Jane Heintzman, whose love and support is infinite.

To my wife Roz, who has been supportive through many years of endless drafts, and who is a life partner in every respect, I offer my endless love and gratitude. And of course to my kids Molly and Theodore, who are the reason why I care about the world and why I want to work hard to see it preserved and made better.

Finally, I close with the caveat that all ideas expressed in this book are my own, and not those of any people or organizations that I am involved with. To those I have written about, I hope that I have fairly portrayed your efforts, and that if I have failed in any way, at a minimum my admiration for your labour has been properly captured.

INDEX

jack pine, 44
James Bay hydroelectric project,
126
Japan
auto industry, 30
and B.C. logging market, 41
energy efficiency, 29
oil consumption, 29–30
R&D, 233
water market, 86
Jimmy Carter Foundation, 199
J. L. Albright Venture Partners,
139
jobs
auto industry, 149, 151
forestry, 40
green markets, 29, 30
natural resources, 22
renewable energy, 30, 138
Johnson Controls, 56
Johnson, Glenn, 111–13, 112n,
115–18

Kashabowie (B.C.), 147
Kenney Dam (B.C.), 46
Kiessling, Greg, 132–34
Kitigawa, Myles, 174
Kitimat (B.C.), 46
Kleiner Perkins (co), 159
Kyoto agreement, 63, 64

Lafarge Cement, 221–22
lakes, 33, 38, 46, 69, 76 (See also
Great Lakes)
Lambeitz, Lionel, 181, 183–86
le grand voyage (canoe ride),
17–19
leadership, 6–7, 239–40, 243
leak detection analysis, 90–91

LEEDS (Leadership in Energy
and Environmental Design),
50, 56, 130
Lennon, John, 15
lignin, 194
lithium-ion batteries, 154, 156
Lloyd, William Forster, 25
Loblaws, 215
lodgepole pine forests. See
mountain pine beetle
epidemic
Lombard, Stuart, 139–41
Loteck Wireless Inc., 50n,
99–101, 102
Lotimer, Jim, 239
Lougheed, Peter, 79, 84, 174
Lovins, Amory, 137–38
low-carbon investment gap,
231–32
low-head hydro projects,
127–31

MacDonald Dettwiler and
Associates, 122
MacDonald, Dr. John, 122–23
Macdonald, John A., 240
Mackenzie, Alexander, 16, 20
Mackenzie River, 16
Mackenzie Valley Pipeline, 126,
178
Mac's Convenience stores, 135
Magee, Bernice, 33, 41–42
Magee, George, 33–34
Maher, Jessica, 184
Mandela, Nelson, 15
Manhattan Project, 56
Manitoulin Island, 71
manufacturing sector, 78, 97,
149–50, 175
manure, 206

world food production, 67, 207,
    209
World Health Organization
    (WHO), 86
World Trade Organization
    (WTO), 83
World Wildlife Fund, 79

XPV Capital, 89

Yahoo!, 226
Yield Protection Technology™,
    220–21
Yingli Green Energy, 231
YouTube, 226

Zenn (electric car), 158–59
Zenn Motor Company, 157, 159
Zenon Environmental, 87–89,
    91, 133
zero-emissions cars. *See* electric
    cars
Zettel, Ted, 215–19
Zoshi, Joshua, 93–94, 96
Zumer, 126

ABOUT THE AUTHOR

ANDREW HEINTZMAN is president and a co-founder of Investeco Capital, the first Canadian investment company focused exclusively on environmental sectors. Andrew is also the Chair of the Premier's Climate Change Advisory Panel for the Province of Ontario. Andrew was co-editor of *Fueling the Future: How the Battle Over Energy Is Changing Everything*, *Feeding the Future: From Fat to Famine*, and *Food and Fuel: Solutions for the Future*. He sits on a number of corporate boards, including Lotek Wireless, Triton Logging, and Horizon Distributors. He is on the board of directors of the Tides Canada Foundation, and the Steering Committee of Sustainable Prosperity. Before Investeco, Andrew was a co-founder and publisher of *Shift* magazine. He lives in Toronto.